The Unwalled City

THE
UNWALLED
CITY *Reconstituting*
the Urban Community

NORTON E. LONG

BASIC BOOKS, INC., PUBLISHERS

NEW YORK   LONDON

Library of Congress Catalog Card Number 72–76903
SBN 465–08898–8
Manufactured in the United States of America
DESIGNED BY THE INKWELL STUDIO

74 75 76   10 9 8 7 6 5 4 3 2

To Jane and to St. Louis
who made this book possible

Preface

"The conventional wisdom of many liberals, that what the cities need most is much more money and more and better programs, may well be hopelessly inadequate. Money and programs would probably help a lot but not unless accompanied by fundamental changes in the politics and management of cities." This quotation appears on the jacket of David Rogers' recent book *The Management of Big Cities*. The author of *110 Livingston Street* has good reason to suspect that the equation of money spent with any measurable quality or quantity of organizational output is both self-serving and suspect. Yet the major emphasis of most of the voices lifted—mayors' and others'—concerning the cities' ills and their remedies is on money, the cities' lack of it, and the urgent necessity of providing more, much more, of it from other governments, the states, and the nation. This book is written from the unconventional and, at least in some quarters, unpopular view that the cities' problems are not primarily due to their lack of money. The perspective of this volume is that major problems of cities stem neither from the inadequacy of their resources nor even—a more debatable point—from their inability to tax such resources as they may have, but from their failure to utilize quite significant resources (now being wasted) in a manner to promote and improve the viability of their local economies.

If there is one thing our experience with foreign aid should have taught us, it is that the only governments and societies that can be helped are those prepared to help themselves. Revenue sharing, the current panacea for the city, is no more likely to produce viable local economies than was foreign aid abroad. Indeed, by providing mayors (including liberal ones like John Lindsay) with an out, the nonsolution, revenue sharing, may, and probably will, postpone their confrontation with the politically painful task of putting their local economic houses in order. This postponement can be costly. The grim picture of Newark as painted by George Sternlieb (in "The City as Sandbox") in the Fall 1971 issue of the *Public Interest* is a warning. The city, as Sternlieb (and this book) sees it, may tend toward such a nonviable local economy—in his terms a "sandbox" for those outside the working economy, in the terms of this volume a reservation or a poor farm downtown.

The growth of the public sector in the city's economy, to the extent that it becomes the dominant source of employment, exacerbates local politics, since the stakes, like those of an underdeveloped country, become those of living from moderately to well if you are on the public payroll, to barely if you are not. Under these circumstances the tenacity and ferocity with which people fight for their vested interests in the public purse become something to behold. To turn this ecology of zero sum games with its calamitous tendency toward stagnation and further degeneration into a rational mutually beneficent system of multiple payoffs becomes more and more beyond the wit, will, and political capacity of such local leadership as we can muster. The tragedy of the growth of the local public sector is that while it provides income to those it employs, it has no necessary connection with increasing the viability of the local economy and, all too often, is so much dead weight dragging it down. While we might all live by taking in one another's washing, we can not all live through the mutual exchange of patent medicines, however well intended and well advertised. If our enormous investment in schools, police, and health results neither in the employability of our youth, nor the safety of our streets, or lowered morbidity, it is a waste of our resources no matter how meritorious its announced objectives. When this investment not only fails in its manifest function, but also produces latent dysfunctions, such as unemployable youth, it can become a cancerous growth.

Cities have financial records; they lack economic accounts. Indeed, most mayors and most urbanists do not even consider the cities as local economies. It is thus not surprising that most view the cities as largely powerless to significantly affect their fate through their own actions. Powerlessness is a self-conception that is not only a fatal and attractive adaptation for the unfortunates of Oscar Lewis' and Lee Rainwater's culture of poverty and for Edward Banfield's *Unheavenly City,* but for otherwise quite powerful and distinguished mayors and civic leaders. Powerlessness is partly self-serving since it means you are blameless for not doing the painful things you might have to do if you seriously wished to produce change in desired directions. Partly, powerlessness is the result of the state of our economics and political science which in different ways have treated the city as trivial in its effects on important aspects of the human condition. Economics, by and large, has derived what it had to say about the local economy from national income shares. It simply doesn't know much about the functioning of local economies, or whether in their unbounded state such economies can be regarded as significant. Wilbur Thompson's urban economics text, the first in this country, is only a few years old. A leading political science student of the city, James Q. Wilson, recently explained our lack of empirical knowledge of the city as stemming from its lack of meaning in our important concerns. Robert Dahl's classic *Who Governs?* takes this view, shared by New Haven's voters, as a matter of course rather than something itself in need of explanation.

This view of the city as trivial is itself far from trivial. Indeed, it is calamitous for it leads the cities' inhabitants and
the cities' leaders alike to expect to accomplish little
through their own efforts and to rest their salvation in outside hands. Such a posture is a recipe for increasing dependency and the conditions leading to dependency. It has
received a classic description in Vidich and Bensman's
Small Town in Mass Society. Unfortunately, the syndrome
that they described as characterizing their small town also
describes many large cities. The cities' leaders and the cities' inhabitants have been taught to believe that the unwalled cities of the nation-state no longer possess significant power over their economic fate. At most they are
local housekeeping agencies who must beg handouts from
superior governments when their revenues fall short and
pinch. They are regarded and regard themselves as without significant power to favorably alter their economic fate
by efforts of their own.

In practice, and as things now stand, this may in fact be
the case. In principle and hopefully in still feasible altered
practice, this need not be the case. Appropriately led, with
a committed coalition of local inhabitants, the existing resources of even our poorest cities could be made to yield a
decisive difference in the lives of their people. Much less
economically promising aggregations of people, Amish and
Black Muslim churches, for example, make most significant
differences in the lives of their members. They do so by
creating the conditions under which resources are effectively and productively used rather than wantonly wasted
or destroyed. An Amish or Muslim school teaches the children entrusted to it to read and to acquire the necessary
habits of discipline to function in a productive economy. It
does this, and in the bargain it does not create a damaged
sense of self-worth or a mindless rebelliousness and indiscipline that predicts marginal or unemployability. It does

this, moreover, with relatively minor resources as compared with even the poorest city. The differences between an Amish or Muslim church and a city are large, but their experiences do point to the central problem—that of effective resource utilization. They also point to something else, the importance of effective resource utilization for the existence of a community in whose interest and by whose authority resources are effectively utilized.

Foreign aid should have taught us that you can not buy any honey with money; that appropriate institutions and motivations must exist, or more and more money can be endlessly wasted on projects with the most attractive labels. This lesson we need to apply to the American city. Another and related lesson needs learning from foreign experience. Nation-building is hard, and its attainment and maintenance cannot be taken for granted. When the prevailing attitude is every man for himself and the devil take the hindmost with little or no national commitment, resources inevitably dissipate. The same is true of cities. City-building and city-rebuilding are far more than the purely physical process our brick and mortar politics of urban renewal has imagined it to be. Indeed, it is questionable whether our politics will ever be able to address the problems of renewing social structure as long as its payoffs are so closely related to brick and mortar.

Turning our cities around is of the greatest moment not only to the cities, but to the nation as well. The rhetoric of urban fiscal woe and its revenue sharing remedy would lead one to suppose that there are a multitude of "sick cities" in a healthy nation from whose wealth a healing balm of money can be extracted. But this is scarcely possible in any fundamental sense. The national economy can not flourish while the local economies that make it up wither. Only because we fail to see the cities as local economies composing the cellular structure of the national economy is this obscure. Can the cities be fiscally sick and economically sound? Such a condition is hardly credible. The cities that are sick are so because too many of their inhabitants are unemployed or underemployed and because too great a part of the investment of their scarce public resources is in public goods and public employment that fails to pay its way by contributing positively to the viability of the local economy. Cities, like countries, unless they are to become dependent satellites of other or larger societies, must pay their way through the exchange of goods and services. This is true even when they become dependent poor farms and Indian reservations, as some are in the process of becoming.

The health of the city is the employment and the upgrading of the employment of its people. As Aristotle wisely said, "one must first live in order to live well." The older city knew that it needs must look to its livelihood if it were to live at all, let alone live well. The contemporary city of the nation state has looked to the nation and market capitalism to insure its economic viability. In an era of rapidly expanding local public goods, these mechanisms have failed. The agony of Newark is a late stage of a generally prevalent disease. The cure for the disease, if cure there be, lies in the rebuilding of the city as a political community whose members, in sufficient degree, accept a common shared fate and empower a leadership to shape that fate so far as it lies in the power of the city. That power may be far more than we now imagine.

N.E.L.

Contents

1

The Unwalled City

THE MODERN CITY is losing its external and formal structure. Internally it is in a state of decay while the new community represented by the nation everywhere grows at its expense. The age of the city seems to be at an end." [1] Don Martindale concludes his prefatory remarks to his edition of Max Weber's essay on *The City* with this melancholy forecast. The forecast would hold more hope for the new, with all our regret for the old, were we more able to discern what significant form of local self-government is ultimately to replace the city of the past. The essence of Weber's view is that when citizens ceased to man the walls, the city ceased to be. This observation, at first sight outrageous, has not only literal sense but a deeper symbolic meaning that points to key phenomena for understanding the city.

For Weber, as Martindale rightly points out, what makes a city is fundamentally its political character. Not any assemblage of men, however numerous and dense their settlement or however tight their economic bonds, but an assemblage of men bound together in a self-governing association is a city. The view is profoundly Greek and political. It denies the quality of city to the cities of the East and to many of the West as well. Perhaps, better understood, even the cities of the East will turn out to have had a more significant political life than is ordinarily supposed. Still, Weber's method of onesidedly forcing the main point has the virtue of casting a strong light on the fundamentals. When Weber places his emphasis on citizens manning walls he calls attention to two vital things: the existence of walls, significant, real boundaries of the city, and the existence of citizens who man them and are ready to risk their lives in defense of the city. The destruction of the walls, the opening of the city, has consequences. Can an unwalled city be meaningfully, symbolically walled? What kind, what depth of loyalty can an unwalled city command from its citizens? Indeed, can it have citizens?

The city of New York is more populous and wealthier than the state of Israel. Yet no one can doubt that the city of New York possesses far less capacity to mobilize men and materials than the state of Israel. Indeed, were this not the case, not only the unity of the state of New York but the unity of the United States itself would be in danger. The modern nation-state came into being by battering down the walls of those quasi–city-states and provinces which, in Hobbes's pungent phrase, were often "worms in the entrails" of its predecessors. Our mode of thinking about the city stems, as does Weber's, from a romantic nostalgia for the Greek city-state and the medieval and Renaissance city. These were cities with walls to be manned and a vibrant, full-blooded life to be lived. In Aristotle's sense they were a species of moral architecture providing a meaningful theater of action for calling into play the potentials of their citizens. According to Sabine,[2] when the Greek city-state gave way to the Hellenistic monarchy men had to grow souls to compensate for their lost citizenship, and the Middle Ages had begun.

The Greek city had the excitement of large and critical affairs, war, and peace. For those of its inhabitants who were full citizens, ruling may have had the same heady attraction that the precincts of power exert in Washington. For others, not of the favored few, the city-state may have presented an aspect more in accord with the sour views of the cynics than with those of philohellenists. The funeral oration of Pericles is spoken to an Athens by our standards highly aristocratic. But what is clearest about the funeral oration is that it would have had no occasion to occur in a dependent city. The persistent power of the Periclean ideal and its reach is illustrated by an admiring reference in Solzhenitzyn's *The First Circle*.[3]

The cities of the Middle Ages and the Renaissance were less completely self-governing than was the classic Greek city-state. Yet they were, in Weber's sense, defense communities, and in most important ways self-governing. They bought their freedom from external control with money and military service that were prices paid for self-determination. Their charters were "liberties," and these liberties were purchased exemptions from royal or baronial control. This is, in its earliest sense, the meaning of home rule. The burgher city of the Middle Ages and early modern times, the predecessor of our own, was a self-governing corporation with its freedom from feudal control fought for and purchased from the countryside and its nobility in alliance, and on occasion in conflict, with nationalizing monarchs. City air makes free, the Germans said, and for the medieval serf the city's walls were the means and the defense of what freedom he could hope for. The tension between city and countryside and the powers of the countryside has continued in our own history, and the alliance of cities and kings has reemerged in the alliance of cities with the national government.

The frontier towns of our own past were defense communities. In the North their Calvinism could combine religious and worldly pursuits in a tight-knit church-state well nigh Greek in character. (Fustel de Coulanges, in his *Cité Antique*,[4] has strongly emphasized the religious nature of the early city.) A secular modernity has paid little heed to the importance of religion and religious associations in creating the social conditions a later market society would take as free gifts of nature. For a long time commercial rivalries gave the competition between American cities for trade routes and territory a character continuous with the past. Not only Boston, New York, Philadelphia, and Baltimore but, as Wade has shown, the cities of the frontier—Lexington, Saint Louis, Louisville, Pittsburgh, and Cincinnati—vied for primacy. Though their conflict lacked the resort to military force of a Venice or a Florence, their merchant princes struggled for markets for themselves and their cities much as did their predecessors.

The commercial city had a commercial regime in the Aristotelian sense, a commercial ethos that lent regime and rulers legitimacy in their own eyes and in the eyes of their fellows. The city had a kind of unity as a family of fellow stockholders in a municipal trading corporation. Even when Calvinism grew dim, the religion of work and sheer Darwinian struggle for survival kept the church-state going as a "we," in competition with the threatening "they" who menaced the common livelihood. This ethos of the mercantile city still holds in many small cities and towns—and in the rhetoric of large cities as well.

The replacement of the merchant city by the manufacturing city undercut the base of economic interests that had attached economic leaders to the city. The boosterism that tied the interests of local merchants to population growth and rising land values was increasingly overshadowed by manufacturers' concern with regional and national markets. Though family concerns continued, and still continue, the older tradition of local merchant patriotism, the logic of the corporate form, and the national market reduced most of these to branch-plant status. Except in headquarters cities, and even there for the most part, the interest of economic leaders goes little beyond the maintaining of a good corporate image. Public relations and those few favors in taxes and utilities that the company requires become the typical embodiment of the local political interest of the corporation.

For a short period in American urban history—from after the Civil War until the turn of the century—owners of manufacturing plants were active in local politics. But from 1900 on, the economic powers became more and more aloof from overt participation in the offices of the city. This is explained partly by their being pushed out by the rising power of the immigrant working class (which their factories had called into being), partly by the incompatibility of the arduous requirements of electioneering with ruling businesses only slightly affected by the routine course of local politics, partly by an increasing sensitivity, which made the rough and tumble of democratic politics distasteful to men accustomed to deference, but primarily because the economic dominants of the manufacturing city did not need a tight grip on local politics to protect and foster their interests.

For the economic dominants the city was unwalled. Should its formal rulers threaten their interests they could and did resort to state governments and to state and federal courts to repel the assault. Failing that, they could always hold over the city the threat or actuality of their flight. For the changed character of the countryside has reduced the city's near monopoly on a favorable business location. As a result, the classic politics of the corporation have become ever more limited—public relations, lobbying, and occasional good works, with a dependence on senior governments and courts backed up by the ultimate weapon of flight. The feasibility of this last recourse must have given Mayor Lindsay a sneaking sympathy for the Berlin Wall when the New York Stock Exchange threatened him with its departure.

Robert Dahl has given what can be taken as an almost ideal typical history of the rulers of an older Eastern city. His study of New Haven, *Who Governs?*,[5] traces the replacement of the congregational oligarchy of gentry, minis-

ters, professionals, and merchants by the rising self-made
men of manufacturing, who in their turn give place to
those he calls the explebes, a new brand of self-made men
who rise to power in local government through their capacity to exploit their personal popularity and the ethnic
and working-class sentiments of the mass electorate. In
Dahl's account the structure of power, which in the beginning was concentrated in the same hands, becomes dif-
fused by the separation of social, economic, and political
power. The hierarchies of society, the economy and the
polity, cease to coincide. This has caused such sociologists
as George Brotz to wonder how and how long a society
could endure with its social, economic, and political hierarchies divided. Is this a house divided against itself that
cannot stand or a pluralistic division of power on whose
competition the free choices of the underlying population
depend?

The picture that Dahl paints can be replicated in other
parts of the country and in Canada as well, except that in
the more recently settled cities, the gentry and the ministry
never had a chance to develop power. There the commercial oligarchy ruled from the beginning. But that apart, the
common course is much the same. The social and economic elite retire from local public office, taking refuge
and doing their duty, as Edward Banfield and James Q.
Wilson point out, in the good works of library boards,
community chests, and welfare.[6] (To this apparent abdication there is perhaps a major exception in the continued
interest in and, at least until recently, control over education by the business and social elite.) The explebes of
Dahl, the technicians of ethnic and electoral politics, take
over the formal governing of the city. Their base, the
source of income and incentives, becomes the fantastically
growing municipal construction and employment that the
dense population of the manufacturing city requires.

For a time, with the progressive movement and the muckraking campaign against bossism and corruption, it seemed as if the business and social elite might stage a return to formal political power in the city, supported by the swelling ranks of a middle class. But in spite of occasional victories in a large city and more enduring conquests in the smaller, the tide of middle-class reform ebbed. Its ebb resulted in part at least from the option in the unwalled city for the middle class to solve its political problems by suburbanizing. In the large city the option to seek a homogenized environment in which to consume residential amenities has increasingly seemed preferable to grappling with the problems of the central city. Not only have large numbers of middle-class people come to the same conclusion, but so, increasingly, have members of the stable working class, and, to the extent suburban residential segregation has permitted it, blacks.

Middle and working classes have followed earlier upper-class migrants beyond the city's boundaries, secure in the knowledge that this separation of place of residence from place of livelihood would impose no loss of job. In fact, given the usual disparity between central city and suburban taxes, the move might and frequently did mean a net gain, despite increased costs of transport. As time passed and suburban numbers swelled, many who had journeyed to work in the city found employment in the shops and firms that had moved to take advantage of the growing affluent population of suburbia and the low-cost land made available by a new transport technology.

The automobile and the truck are frequently regarded as the villains that destroyed the homeostatic balance of the older city. Certainly the new transport technology produced major changes in land values and the pattern of settlement. By tremendously reducing the costs of moving men and materials, the automobile and the truck opened up low-priced suburban land for residential and industrial use. It struck at the older city in two related ways: (1) It made it possible for many of the affluent, and eventually even those of modest means, to settle in the suburbs, thereby removing sources of high tax yield and civic competence from the city. (2) It made possible the departure of businesses to the outer ring.

Had the city's loss of population and business been accompanied by a compensating decline in its costs, the change might have seemed beneficial to those who had long deplored urban densities. Real estate speculators who had made their money through urban population growth might have been the only ones to seriously mourn the city's stabilization at a desirable density. Unfortunately, the decline in the city's human and business population has been unaccompanied by compensating reduction in its costs. Indeed, quite the reverse: As the city lost population and tax base, its costs increased. The fashionable explanation for this phenomenon has been the change in the city's population and industry mix. What has been going on has not been just a proportionate outmigration of the city's previous mix but the kind of outflow and inflow that have combined to homogenize the city's residents and businesses downward on the income-producing scale and upward on the service-cost–demanding scale. This is the fashionable explanation for the present plight of the older city and suburb. It commands a considerable volume of evidence to substantiate if not confirm it.

Jay Forrester of M.I.T. has modeled a systems' explanation of the city's decline in his *Urban Dynamics*.[7] There he shows how, given a fixed area of empty land, it is possible to simulate a process that will lead from new industry, with managers, professionals, and employed workers and with new upper-class, middle-class, and working-class housing, to an urban mix of mature and declining businesses, under- and unemployed workers, and old and blighted housing. The process in his judgment is exacerbated by the misguided attempts of politicians to alleviate the condition of the poor, the unemployed, and the underemployed. Yet these policies only serve to concentrate the poor, increase the demand for low rent, blighted housing, and, by burdening the affluent and mobile businesses, encourage the latter's departure from the city. At the same time, they discourage new business and new construction and the inmigration of the productively employed.

Mayor Collins of Boston, who consulted with Forrester on his book, must have had mixed feelings as to its message. On the one hand, he may have felt reassured that a policy of urban renewal designed to exchange the city's poor for returning members of the middle class and the marginal small businesses and honky tonks of Scolley Square for central-city office space was correct. On the other hand, he may have wondered whether this was not some of the well-meant but inept systemic interference that Forrester deplores. It is not quite clear from Forrester's book or from other systems and equilibrium-type economic writing what if anything besides laissez-faire is good for the city. Certainly one might suppose that policies that concentrate the poor and drive out both productive employment and the productively employed are neither in the interests of the city, whatever these may be, nor ultimately in the interests of the poor, the ostensible beneficiaries. Forrester seems to suggest, without saying so, that the older city should sternly follow policies that will decant its poor to the suburbs or elsewhere and encourage the productively employed and productive employment to remain within and even settle within its boundaries. This is not easy to do even if the state or national government—or the outside society—would permit it.

Perhaps it is not just the perversity of politicians

demagogically—or just plain misguidedly—seeking to relieve the misery of the poor that occasions the downward homogenization of the older city. In much, though by no means all, of the country the unwalled city is surrounded by a wall of suburban incorporation, which excludes it from open land precisely where most of the new growth of residence and industry can be expected to occur. Where in the past the city had undeveloped land and room for new growth within its borders, it is now built up. It can only find room for new growth by an expensive process of the assemblage and demolition of built-up property. Being largely built up, the older city has the greatest concentration of old and obsolete structures that are incurring rising maintenance costs and is noncompetitive with the new facilities built outside it. Any built-up limited area would face a similar problem of the downward mobility of its aging, obsolescing real estate. The city has until recently had a fountain of youth to overcome the seemingly inexorable forces of aging. Until the truck and the automobile, and in some cities in spite of them, central-city locations have been of such high economic value that it paid to demolish still useful standing structures and replace them with new ones. The revolution in transport undercut the city's locational edge. Walled in by suburban incorporation, it could not expand to open land. Without its previous locational advantage its real estate was as subject to obsolescence as any consumer or producer. The novelty was that the full force of the transport revolution only became apparent after World War II.

Those cities whose boundaries have been expansible because state policy has favored annexation have suffered a different fate. They have been able to participate effectively in new growth and to plan their future. The downward mobility of the older central city, hemmed in from the area of new growth, has extended to the older suburb, and for similar reasons. This downward mobility would seem as much the inevitable fate of old plants and old houses as of old trucks and old automobiles. Some few houses and automobiles may hold and increase their value as antiques; many more may hold their value and limit the rate of decline by appropriate levels of maintenance. Indeed, as in the used-car market, old houses like old cars may find their value favorably affected by the rising costs and prices of the new. Such is less likely to be the case of stores and, particularly, factories. Here technological change must almost inevitably render the older structures obsolescent and high cost.

But the grim picture of a built-up city with nowhere to go but down once changes in transport technology have destroyed its locational edge is too simple. It neglects other assets the city might possess that would give it continuing pulling power even when its transportation advantage had disappeared. The city is a store of human as well as purely physical capital. It is a complex of institutions, government, schools, hospitals, and amenities. All these can give it a going-concern value that favorably alters the prospect of otherwise downward mobile real estate. Evanston, Illinois, a dated middle-class suburb of the 1890's, with huge mansions, expensive to maintain in a day of high servant and service costs, has held up despite its real estate because good schools, good police, and good government have made strong middle-class families happy to bear the added burden of older housing.

Wilbur Thompson, in his pioneering study of urban economics,[8] concludes that the best investment a city could make is in its manpower. This represents a major advance over the previous conventional wisdom bound up in the brick-and-mortar approach of urban renewal. The possession of a skilled and competent labor force could be a powerful locational asset. Even if members of the labor force had to go elsewhere to work, it would be better for the city that they be employed elsewhere than unemployed or underemployed in the city. A policy of effectively investing in the employability of all elements of its population would seem the most likely means of reducing dependency and crime to a minimum and maximizing the utilization of the city's human resources. Such a policy seems such self-evident good sense that it seems incredible that it should not have been followed. It constitutes the most hopeful though unsuccessful initiative of the Nixon administration.

It might seem at first sight that precisely such a strategy had been adopted by the American city. The greatest investment of our local governments has been in education. Until recently taxpayers have accepted ever heavier demands made in the name of education without more than a whimper. But now, as David Rosenbaum of *The New York Times* points out in "See. See the School. It is Broke," [9] taxpayers are in full revolt, and schools are in desperate financial straits. In part, this results from the general inflation of government costs that has finally run into a stone wall of resistance. As Lyle Fitch, former New York City administrator, notes, "Compensation of general government employees rose 72% over the decade, keeping pace with the high flying construction industry." [10] But even more serious than the cost of inflation is the growing suspicion that the investment in education is not paying off, that it may be an expensive social patent medicine of little real medicinal value.

U.S. Commissioner of Education Marland [11] has remarked that much of our education prepares neither for college nor for a job. To which it has been replied that only a philistine would fail to appreciate that education exists for education's sake. A cynic, or perhaps just a realist, would see in this the claim that education should exist

14

for the sake of the educators, not for the sake of the pupils it processes or for the taxpayers who pay its bills. The case of education is fairly typical of all the municipal investments, whether they be in police, fire, welfare, or health. The problem is one of the typical displacement of concern from product to process and processors. The displacement is made easier and more inevitable by the product and its utility being treated as either inappropriate or impossible to measure. In practice this has meant that we have measured educational outputs by inputs with no independent assessment of the cost effective relation, if any, between them.

James Coleman's report, *Equality of Educational Opportunity,*[12] is now some five years old, and though it has been sharply criticized, it remains largely unrebutted and, perhaps worse, unheeded. Coleman's study of standard tests shows little relation between conventional educational inputs and objectively measurable outputs. These latter are presumably to be taken on faith in the expert judgment of the educators. With the extraordinary increases in educational costs this gets harder to do, especially when it becomes clear that the economists' assurance of the productivity of our educational investment is open to serious question. Associate Dean of Columbia University School of Business Ivar Berg has written a book, *Education and Jobs, The Great Training Robbery,*[13] that casts doubt on the conventional economic wisdom that links education with income via the assumed intervening variable of increased productivity. What Dean Berg's research seems to show is that there is little evidence that educational training is at all well related to either job requirements or job performance. Instead, the personnel people of industry have used educational credentials as a screening device and a cop-out to avoid the responsibility for formulating more rational and testable selection requirements.

This cop-out has had a disastrous impact on the youth of the inner city, and in other places as well. Though the city has lost jobs to the suburban ring, and though its job mix is less favorable than in times past, the actual imbalance between the number of jobs presently existing in many cities and the number of people in those cities does not add up to a scarcity of jobs. It does add up to the oft-noted and oft-deplored fact that for all but the dirty, low-pay, and casual jobs the educational credentials required are far beyond those possessed by most of the people now residing in the cities. This is a more serious mismatch than the more generally complained of fiscal mismatch between the city's financial needs and its financial resources. In fact, this mismatch is far more the reason for the fiscal mismatch than vice versa. What is most calamitous for the city is that the mismatch between its existing decent jobs and the educational credentials for most of those now residing in the city is accepted as a fact of nature, subject to little or no improvement by a course of purposive human action.

Dean Berg points out that, almost alone among our institutions, the armed forces have had the interest and have shown the ability to train the hard core of the city's seemingly uneducable youth for jobs of considerable complexity and skill. Dean Berg may be overly sanguine as to the actual cost effectiveness of the military's educational programs for the hard core. There are the unkind who find in the military's efforts and reputed success more of public relations than actual measurable performance, particularly imitable performance. Be that as it may, Dean Berg's account of the military's action suggests a logic that could account for success where others fail. He suggests that the workings of the draft and the attitudes of middle-class draftees have made the bottom of the manpower pool attractive to the military, at least as a source of combat troops. Where others have been interested in training for their own financial gain, without real concern for the actual employability of those they train, the interest of the military in training has an enlightened self-interest—a concern with the employment of those they train. Such a motivation might predict a far higher degree of success than that associated with conventional education.

What this suggests is something that some central schools are now discovering: The separation of education from the world of work has been a mixed blessing at best. When the little red schoolhouse was the rule, vocational education was near at hand in the family or on the neighbor's farm. The separation of the world of work, and in consequence of meaningful adult roles and the chance to participate in them, from the world of education had not yet taken place. Where the older union of the two worlds persists, as with the Amish, a seventeen-year-old girl with no more than a high school education teaches the three r's in a one-room school to pupils who learn and by all standard tests do as well as those taught in the best financed and most highly accredited schools. We need perhaps not wholly emulate the Amish to learn from their model. Indeed, under even less promising circumstances, the Black Muslims achieve similar success. It is not the saving in expense that commends our own earlier education, though that is no small item. The separation of the world of work from the world of education has disoriented both youth and education from a healthy and functional relation to the larger society.

Youth, immured in a school system purposefully segregated from the outside society and deprived of the opportunity to participate in adult roles and gainful employment until long after it has reached a biological and psychological competence to do so, has been led to form a counterculture of its own. An education conspicuously and self-consciously avoiding contamination with the world of work and denying that it is in any important way to be judged by the employability of its pupils becomes a Veblenian object of conspicuous social consumption of high honorificence and low utility. Curiously, middle-class and even business leaders, the unions, and the educational establishment have conspired to produce the result. Middle-class education has become ever increasingly college oriented, and the colleges, despite the land grant tradition, have turned more and more to the Oxford and Cambridge model with a powerful thrust toward the graduate school, the German university, and the crowning goal of the doctorate. Abram Flexner's *Universities, American, English, German,*[14] codified the aspiration. The unions had a humbler role in the expedient pursuit of job protectionism to keep youth off the labor market and to control access to the trades through the apprentice programs. The educational establishment, through the alliance of insulated departments of education, schools of education, curriculum and certification requirements and associations, developed a monopoly on the provision of education and its assessment. Insofar as the output of the whole structure has received any test, it has been through the college gatekeepers, whose norms bear an unexamined relation to the needs of the colleges and the society.

Christopher Jencks, reviewing the Coleman study three years after its issue, concluded that it was probably correct in its major thrust that school inputs bore little significant relationship to school outputs as measured by standard tests.[15] As he points out, though major emphasis is placed on academic achievement, the importance of this achievement for success or failure in life remains to be demonstrated. Thus he urges,

Despite much popular rhetoric, there is little evidence that academic competence is critically important to adults in most walks of life. If you ask employers why they won't hire dropouts, for example, or why they promote certain kinds of people and not others, they seldom complain that dropouts can't read. Instead they complain that dropouts don't get to work on time, can't be counted on to do a careful job, don't get along with others in the plant or office, can't be trusted to keep their hands out of the till and so on. Nor do the available survey data suggest that the adult success of people from disadvantaged backgrounds depends on their intellectual skills. If you compare black men who do well on the Armed Forces Qualifications Test to those who do badly, for example, you find that a black man who scores as high as the average white still earns only about two-thirds what the average white earns. Not only that, he hardly earns more than the average black. Even for whites, the mental abilities measured by the A.F.Q.T. account for less than a tenth of the variation in earnings.

Jencks concludes that the "middle-class virtues" of self-discipline and self-respect are what is most needed and what in a clumsy way the slum school tries to do, as has for similar reasons the parochial school. "It is the schools' failure to develop these personal characteristics," says Jencks, "not its failure to teach history or physics or verbal skill that lies behind the present upheavals in the schools. And it is this failure to which reformers should be addressing themselves."

At a meeting in the office of the mayor of Saint Louis, a representative of the Missouri State Employment Service asked, "What do you do with kids who fall asleep during a job interview, spit on the floor, can't spell their own names or the name of the street on which they live and can't locate the place they are to apply for work on a map?" [16] And an official of the Saint Louis school system remained apparently sympathetically silent. Yet the Saint Louis school system is given high marks by the educational expert of the *Post Dispatch,* possibly for keeping or being kept out of partisan politics, which the paper rates as a great virtue. The blue ribbon school board shares this view despite the dissent not only of lower-class blacks but of middle-class whites and blacks, who massively withdraw from the city.

Clearly a school system that not only fails to achieve literacy but fosters a mindless rebelliousness and lack of discipline and self-respect among its students is an expensive luxury for a run-down and near-bankrupt city. Docility in some middle-class and most black militant circles is a dirty word, especially if it amounts to the capacity and willingness to shape up and work for the man. But employers, white or black, are and have to be interested in hiring employees who are susceptible to discipline and are teachable. In a tight labor market they, and more particularly their foremen, may put up with quite a bit; in a soft labor market indocility is a recipe for un- and underemployment. Some public relations showcase operations may make a point of proving their ability to employ the hard core, but in most competitive situations it simply does not pay. Over time, and not too much time, for most it has to pay.

It is a tragedy for lower-class blacks, and lower-class kids generally, that their education is modeled after that of the middle class. This is especially true since if Berg is correct, and Jencks too for that matter, the academic skills are unrelated to success in life. This does not mean, of course, that the academic credentials are unrelated. Quite the contrary, they are. And lower-class and other people observing the close relation between credentials received and income attained have quite naturally desired to obtain this passport to middle-class status for their offspring. Unfortunately, in the absence of meaningful skills the mass production of credentials can only cheapen their scarcity value. It leads to a familiar scheme of rating the credentials so that in Orwell's sense some degrees are more equal than others. The effort to homogenize urban education as a means of observing the society's poorly observed equality norm through equalizing educational opportunity has had unfortunate consequences for all concerned. The middle class, for this reason among others, leaves the city, and the poor are left with a watered-down version of a middle-class education.

On asking the Missouri State Employment Service what skills are taught in the schools that would favorably predict employability, the only course mentioned was stenography. Now Jencks may well be right that the most important things a slum school can teach are self-discipline and self-respect, but these may be hard to teach through a curriculum that is perceived by students and teachers alike as leading nowhere. An experiment in Saint Louis, and one that is going on elsewhere, gives promise of greater success. Some nine companies, including several banks, oil companies, downtown stores, the *Post Dispatch*, Southwestern Bell, and Ralston Purina, are engaged in a work-study program. It is pitifully small, enrolling some 300 students. But it does seem to attract and hold students, who do succeed on the job and in their studies. Southwestern Bell reports a retention rate of some 82 per cent, higher than the rate for hires at the gate.[17]

Despite the success of the program, it has remained confined to the nine companies. The bridge between school and work has been highly beneficial both to motivate students by enabling them to earn and participate in a respected adult role and to show them the practical value of at least some of their studies. Not least among the beneficiaries have been the teachers, who regained a sense of achievement in teaching students who learned in a situation where learning had a demonstrable payoff. Nevertheless, despite accolades from the participating companies and the press, the program has never received the support required to give it real impact. The education establishment, though not the superintendent, regard the program as a threat to the liberal education that is their specialty. Principals feel that pupils enrolled in the program mean a loss of the best motivated students from ordinary school classes. In short, the bulk of the education establishment has a scoring system that sees in the work-study program a danger rather than an opportunity.

Most employers just simply can not be bothered. Though they vehemently deplore youth crime, drug addiction, and welfare, they fail to connect these evils to the lack of any effective bridge between education and jobs. Not realizing that a school system that is a staircase leading nowhere must be an expensive and counterproductive waste of funds, they miss the connection between their employment practices, the schools, and the problems of the city. It is ironic that the college gatekeepers rather than the personnel men of industry exercise what influence there is on the city's schools and that inner-city counselors know more about college requirements than job requirements. Given Ivar Berg's findings, it is not surprising that personnel men of industry should have done little to relate the curriculum of the schools to job requirements. It appears that they themselves have little notion of what these requirements are and have hidden behind educational credentials as predictors of job success. Work study shows that even in the limited state of industry's knowledge something better could be done.

Unfortunately the relation of schools to work and the importance of that relation to the ills of the city—crime, poverty, and dependency—remain no one's business. Rhetorical recognition may be given to the desirability of improving the relation, its lack may be denounced, steps to improve it may be commended, but by and large no one with power, as the existing scoring and information system works, has a sufficient interest in bucking the forces that engender the perpetuation of the status quo. A newly elected mayor of Boston might well be told by his Harvard advisors that his best course for improving the condition of the inhabitants of Boston would be to increase the employability of the city's youth and that this would mean a reform of the school system. But a newly elected mayor of Boston would first tell his advisors that he does not control the school system, that it is the job of the school board, that to control the school board would mean taking on the educational establishment in a battle he might not win; and even if he did win, there is a good chance that any payoff in the increased employability of the city's youth would not occur in time to do him any good. A mayor of Boston, or of most other places, would be hoping to do those things that, within his limited political means, had immediate promise of furthering his next move up the political ladder. A black mayor of Gary with nowhere else to go can have the courage of despair and race pride to enter into an accountability contract with a California firm and antagonize the educational establishment. He may well conclude he has nothing to lose. But it would be folly to count on such a response from even a black mayor. And accountability contracts may produce academic skills, but the skills and jobs have to be put together to accomplish much. However, it is no small gain for a city to have a mayor courageously interested in the education of its youth.

It is at first sight odd that education, which the economists have heralded as our major public investment and the investment most accountable for our postwar prosperity, should be treated so casually and its effectiveness, despite its massive cost, taken on faith. But as Coleman's and Dean Berg's studies indicate, we know precious little about the relation between educational inputs and outputs. We do not know whether and to what degree inputs account for any significant differences in performance on standard

23

academic tests, and, more importantly, we do not know whether academic credentials are positively related to job requirements and performance. We may suspect that for the central city and the older suburb these credentials serve as an unjustifiable form of job discrimination, keeping their youth from jobs they could be made to perform. If Jencks is right, and the odds are he is, a sentimental and ideological, well meant but counterproductive liberalism has undermined the discipline of inner-city and parochial schools that may have been the source of the most useful lesson their pupils learned. A constructive rebelliousness might be a highly useful thing to learn, though difficult to teach; a mindless indiscipline, self-indulgence, and confusion of slogans with thought can be a disaster for those who acquire the habit and those who become their victims.

Conceivably, education might serve not only as an investment for the city in the employability of its youth and thus in the creation of a prime locational asset—a well-trained, competent labor force—but in improving the effectiveness of its population in other ways. Among our most expensive outlays is that for health. Almost all of this goes for the clinical practice of medicine rather than for the prevention of disease, accidents, and other sources of bodily harm. Preventive medicine, public health, is an additional and alternative resource to the after-the-fact clinical repair of damage. Perhaps nowhere better than in the schools could the rudiments of an effective health culture be disseminated. A knowledge of personal hygiene, maternal and prenatal health, well-baby care, and nutrition would be a major improvement in the capacity of large parts of the city and even suburban population to improve their lives. The failure of education to exploit this possibility is attributable to the scoring systems of schools of education at the universities, state departments of education, schools and school boards, the medical profession, and political and civic leadership. The cost benefits are apparent, the opportunity is there, but the sustained incentive for appropriate action is lacking.

The city, though a municipal corporation, is not run as a cooperative for the efficient utilization of its resources for the welfare of its members. Part of the problem is that its members are citizens and inhabitants rather than stockholders. The civic culture does not provide them with a conception of what dividends they might expect from a well-run city. The conception of the city as a cooperative for the improvement and development of the capacities and lives of its inhabitants is at odds with the doctrine of laissez-faire and a national capitalism that has turned local citizens into consumers and so many free-floating factors of production to be assembled and disassembled by the forces of the national market. The older conception of the walled city as a shared common enterprise has been weakened by the breaching of its walls and its transformation into an open economy. The nation-state has increasingly insisted that national citizens, even noncitizens, be accorded all or almost all the rights and privileges accorded local citizens.

What is the point of belonging to an organization that all may join and none need join to enjoy all its privileges? The loyalty and commitment such an organization can command seem highly limited. The city of New York is not the state of Israel. Under these circumstances it is not surprising that the city becomes a site among other sites looked at by mobile consumers as a bundle of real estate amenities and profit opportunities to be more or less coolly evaluated in comparison with its rivals. In a celebrated article,[18] Ostrom, Tiebout, and Warren challenge the conventional wisdom that sees the metropolitan area as a dysfunctionally fragmented community lacking a common government to give it needed coordination; they make a case for the metropolitan area as a rather well-organized market for a variety of desired real estate uses. In this view, cities, towns, villages, special districts, and other governments are treated as if they were so many governmental firms responding to the market forces of citizen choices expressed by voting with the ballot or more often with the feet.

Though our sentimental attachment to the Greek ideal of the city is great, it is idle not to recognize the enormous advance that national market capitalism has made in the human condition. It was mentioned earlier that the glory of the Greek city-state was to the cynics, who represented perhaps the views of an underlying population, a veneer covering a mass of misery. The keen-eyed and cool-headed students of antiquity who framed the American constitution knew that the glittering republics of antiquity had paid for their intense civic life with endemic class war and that their civic lives proved too often "nasty, brutish and short." They sought by diffusing the effects of faction over large territories and checking it through layers and divisions of government to break the force of faction and combine what had been thought uncombinable—liberty with stable government. In the event, they have proved more successful than they dared dream.

Until recently, despite recessions and wars, American society has seemed a huge success. Race relations apart, and perhaps even here in the absolute condition of the Negro if not the relative, few societies anywhere have achieved such quantitative abundance for most of the many. Kermit Gordon, in his introduction to *Agenda for the Nation*,[19] the political and economic testament of the Kennedy-Johnson intellectuals, thoughtfully reviewed the manifold blessings of the society and then recognized that despite these blessings much was amiss. Poverty amid unparalleled affluence seemed more offensive than ever. Race discrimination despite and because of progress seemed less bearable. The very wealth of the society was choking it with its own waste in the air, the water and on the land. And worst of all, a youth undisciplined by scarcity, bored with affluence, and lacking a spiritual discipline to give it purpose and direction had significant leadership in rejecting the values of its elders. Crime and drug addiction were alarmingly on the increase. Despite all efforts physical blight and decay were spreading from the inner city to the older suburb and elsewhere. Some, such as Edward Banfield, found little amiss but the rhetorical exaggerations of critics. Others wondered whether the built-in stabilizers, the homeostatic principles of market capitalism, could by themselves save the cities from stagnation, decay, and decline. Could the market work? Will it be allowed to work? Can it be made to work?

It is difficult for those who subscribe to a public-choice mechanism of operating the public goods market to explain failure in other terms than untoward human intervention in an otherwise beneficent logical machine. The metropolitan area, which has emerged as the overwhelmingly dominant form of settlement in the nation, is an anticity. Where the city was, at least in legal theory, a corporation rather than a market, a government that required consciously to formulate a public interest, the metropolitan area is an urban agglomeration, a labor market, a housing market, and much else without a common government short of state or nation. To the extent this area had a common interest, it would have to be the resultant working of private market forces and the public market forces with the interaction of their governments. As Robert Wood said of his suburbs in *1400 Governments*,[20] they adapt to market forces rather than adapting them to purposes of their own. The classical economists' theory of the market is a logical device through which the self-interest of the actors, through their interaction in the market, produces an individually unintended, collectively beneficent result. Could such a device apply to a system of competitive coexistence among governments sharing a metropolitan area?

The classical economists' conception of the market is a useful intellectual tool. It provides a model of a set of variables interacting in specified ways to produce a desirable result. Like all useful tools that have been discovered in human history, it may become an object of worship rather than of critical appreciation and improvement. As an object of worship it becomes radically incorrigible, untestable, and hence potentially maleficent. We worshipped at the shrine of the self-regulating economy before the Great Depression. Many still think that had we worshipped it faithfully enough our lot would have been better. In the event, that theory remains untested by practice and perhaps untestable. It was the merit of Keynes, among other things, to give logical demonstration to how starvation could come to the banana plantation and how the economy could stabilize at stagnation levels rather than at those of full employment. Some such Keynesian analysis may be needed of the supposed homeostatically beneficent properties of the metropolitan market of governments. To give that market its due, when Charles Haar and his associates of the M.I.T.-Harvard Joint Center of Metropolitan Studies set out to discover what the ill consequences of the sorry state of metropolitan planning were, they found that the system that had developed somehow managed to meet its problems.[21] Perhaps its performance was less than ideal, but, to use the economists' term, it satisficed.

It is the merit of the economists and the recently developing school of public-choice theorists that they make explicit a set of relatively clear and unambiguous definitions and proceed to draw the logical conclusions they entail. This has resulted in Anthony Downs's producing more interesting and, in principle, testable hypotheses about politics than do most political scientists. Using the concepts of scarcity, self-interest, rationality, and methodological individualism, one can go a surprisingly long way, as has Robert Bish in his *Public Economy of Metropolitan Areas.*[22] This and other works in the public-choice field provide a useful alternative perspective to the conventional wisdom of urbanology typified in the C.E.D. pamphlet on reorganizing local government and the academic literature on metropolitan reform.[23] In this view the metropolitan area is an array of choices for the individual and a field of competition and cooperation for the governments that exist within it. If the assumptions are correct, the self-interest of the actors in the field of intergovernmental competition might be expected to produce the same individually unintended collective beneficence as that of an economic market. The officials of the cities, like the management of firms, would compete and combine as their interest dictated. The citizen consumer would evalute the alternative bills of fare and accommodations provided by the range of competing municipal hotels and select the one best fitting his taste and his purse. Like Miami hotelkeepers, mayors and city managers would compete to attract the custom trade, the paying guests, and avoid if they could the low status and the deadbeat. By providing this array of choice the citizen consumer is freed from the monopolistic coercion of a single city, and the city is kept responsive and on its toes by its competition.

It is easy to wax ironic over the public choice model of the metropolitan area, but for that matter it is easy to do the same over the abstractions of the economist. Like any other kit of tools, the test is in their practical utility. Thus far the literature about the city and the metropolitan area has been largely devoid of analytical concepts. Argument has scarcely risen above the level of abuse and affective rhetoric. If cognitive competence is the key to successful practice, the subject needs to move from the present level of legalism, conventional wisdom, and feeling tone to one that has more possibility of an advance in explanatory theory and the development of a capacity to measure changes in significant dimensions of the human condition. The beginning of wisdom in attempting to move in this direction is methodological individualism. Simply put, this implies making one's judgment of good or bad in terms of what happens to concrete, observable people and seeking to account for what happens through the observable behavior of concrete people. It is this stance that gives great attraction to the attempt of the public-choice school to use the methods of economics as a means of understanding the political economy of the city, the metropolitan area, the state, and the nation. Its tools will not solve all problems, but they make possible a promising start and one that has the immeasurable merit of permitting and even demanding corrigibility by the facts.

What is sought is a model for a set of institutions and their interaction whose structure would have concrete, observable benefits for people built into it. The city of the past had its virtues as compared with the countryside of the past. But the city of the past became a rotten borough, often a machine-controlled enterprise that served to exploit rather than serve its citizens. The breaching of the cities' walls by national market capitalism gave rein to a new and greater freedom than that of the city whose air once made serfs free. This freedom existed in a new community, the community of the nation and perhaps the state. Whether enough of the old community of the city could survive has been questioned. Whether the state or the nation can or will provide viable substitutes are equally important questions.

The city in the open nonpolity of the metropolitan area is something different from what it once was. State citizenship and national citizenship have not taken the place of local citizenship. Though the city is the legal creature of the state it is not the delegate arm of a functioning state community, much less of a national community. The metropolitan area is not a consciously chosen market of governments, chosen as a device to implement the consciously considered choice of a state community through its government. It is a historic creation like the economic market itself, and like the market before it, it is now receiving theoretical justification and understanding of its existence. The metropolitan area as a market provides coordination without planning. If the institutions that comprise it are appropriately set up, the self-interest of their governing actors should lead them to a pattern of interaction that will better meet the needs of individuals than any likely form of metropolitan planning. The metropolitan area, unlike the city, will have no common government short of state or nation. Like any other institution, its fruits will have to be judged in terms of measurable consequences in the lives of the people who inhabit it.

As Robert Bish maintains, the critics of the existing state of affairs of metropolitan areas contrast them with the presumed results of an omniscient and benevolent form of centralized planning. This is a solution drawn from Plato and dear to the hearts of planners, academics, businessmen, and other potential philosopher-kings. Bish finds that this line of reasoning usually runs, as Plato's, to benevolent despotism. It leaves unexplained how the public interest of the metropolitan area comes to be known by the experts who act in its name and what assurance the public, whose private interests are repressed, has that the public interest is other than so often is the case, the interests of rulers masquerading under a fine name. In this view the metropolitan area is an advance in the human condition from the city of the past. To seek to encompass it in some urban governmental form would be to create one more New York with worse, not fewer, problems than existed before. This view and the logic of the metropolitan area where most of us now live need to be explored. This rather than the city of the past is where most of us now live and will live. What it means, what needs doing about it, and what it portends for the existing urban forms are our next concern.

2

*Metropolitan Areas:
Communities without
Governments?*

THE PROPENSITY of a middle-class society to consume a major part of its income in the public sector is a fairly recent development. Whereas the rich could meet their needs with five-acre lots, private hospitals, and private schools, the middle class and even the more affluent members of the working class have found a public goods-producing "cooperative" a more effective device for attaining similar ends. Consumer goods that used to be produced in the private sector and rationed by the private market have come to be produced by the public sector for an increasingly middle-class society. The metropolitan area, as public-choice theorists have come to see it, can be viewed as a governmental market for the varied production and distribution of once private goods.

Interesting consequences flow from the replacement of private market distribution by public market distribution. In the private market people with unequal incomes necessarily have unequal effective demands, whatever their needs. In a public market, however, there is a problem: how to give recognition to economically unequal citizens who are legally politically equal and thus formally entitled to make equal demands. The metropolitan area has made possible the provision of unequal qualities and quantities of public goods to formally equal citizens. It is an effective device for the segregation of consumption of public goods.

The older city has always had good and bad neighborhoods, some neighborhoods where the garbage was picked up twice a week and some where people were lucky if it was picked up at all. Clunker cars adorn some streets and lots abound with rubbish. Some schools are known as good. Teachers, if they can, transfer to them; parents, if they care, try to enroll their children in them. Knowledge-able real estate men will recommend the purchase of prop-erty in such and such a school district and in such and such a parish. Prostitutes, drug addicts, criminals, and de-viants will be shunted into other areas, compounding the problems of those whose incomes or whose racial and so-cial status make residence there inevitable. This is the "airtight cage" of which Martin Luther King spoke and about which Joseph Lyford wrote a book.[1] It indicates that, with all its change, the older city still retains its vari-ety. But change has come, and though neighborhood de-marcations still exist, they have become blurred. The good schools for the middle and stable working classes have been attacked and infiltrated. Police policy, which together with realtors and banks sought—and achieved—the geo-graphic segregation of the "good" and the likely "bad" peo-ple, has fallen victim to civil rights, the rise of minority power, and interference from without.

For the city has been under siege, both by those within and those without, to live up to an equality norm in the treatment of its inhabitants. Often, of course, the demand is made by people who are themselves quite unprepared to live with the consequences of their demands being met. The most frequent reasons given by those leaving the city or by those refusing to take up residence there are schools and security. The schools are no longer thought to be of a quality that ensures the career or college of their pupils; their increasingly democratic composition, moreover, ren-ders them doubtfully safe. This latter concern shades di-rectly into the general fear of crime in the streets. Assaults, purse-snatchings, robbery are thought far more likely in the city than in the suburbs. Add the liability of higher taxes to poor schools and inadequate security, and the city's public goods take on the appearance of poor quality and high price. Given the mobility of the automobile is there any reason to come or to stay? For an increasing number within and without the answer is no.

The array of neighborhoods that used to exist within the city is now projected outside and frequently incorporated in anything from postage-stamp subdivisions to fair-sized bedroom municipalities and industrial enclaves. Thus, while the city has been pressed to homogenize so as to provide its citizens a more equal fare of public goods and permit its inhabitants to freely roam its streets, the metropolitan area has become a rich smorgasbord of land uses to meet the tastes and purses of a highly varied public. From the economists' perspective this wide range of choice is a major advance in consumer welfare, which enhances his power to discriminate from among the bundle of public goods those whose quality and cost best suit his needs and means. Certainly it is hard to deny that a wide range of choice is better than no choice at all. It would be instructive if we knew precisely what, beyond a house and a journey to work—at prices in money and time—were being purchased. For many other goods produced for it, the suburban public goods market may be as—and no more— rational as the private sector. Few consumers are rational by the standards of Consumers' Union, and few advertisers tout their wares in a fashion that satisfies Ralph Nader. The Happy Valleys and Honeymoon Roosts of suburbia are probably chosen no more irrationally—or produced in any more slovenly a fashion—than many of the products in the private sector.

What one would like to know are the consequences of this choice mechanism for the lives of people. Clearly a public goods market such as the metropolitan area rations its goods in the same way as the private sector, namely, by price. The very municipal homogenization that is one of its claims to efficiency spells segregation by income. In fact,

37

as such public-choice theorists as Robert Bish have pointed out, the smaller the group for whom the municipal bundle of public goods is designed, the better it can be packaged to meet the life style and means of the group. From this perspective "postage-stamp suburbs" becomes a term of approbation rather than abuse.

Often this kind of suburb has contrived to have the best of both worlds of scale. Take Los Angeles' Lakewood Plan for example. Lakewood, an incorporated city with no services of its own, contracts with the County of Los Angeles for the full bill of fare. It thus gains such advantages of scale as Los Angeles county's size permits along with the social homogeneity of its own restricted numbers. Many other municipalities have followed Lakewood's lead. They have thus pioneered the middle- or upper-income cooperative municipal club with a government that has been stripped down to a public goods purchasing agency. Inasmuch as they always have the options of furnishing their own services, contracting with private entrepreneurs (or, in some cases, other municipalities and governmental agencies), or jointly producing the service with sister cities, they are not at the mercy of the county. The threatened exercise of these options hangs over the heads of the county's service-producing departments and should stimulate a cost effectiveness unlikely under less competitive conditions.

There is certainly a great deal to be said in favor of separating the production of public goods from decisions concerning their consumption. Employee unions and professional guilds exercise a formidable decision-making power in many cities. Because they frequently have the interest, the numbers, and the power to make a greater political impact than any other group in the city, it is a strong mayor indeed who will do more than temporize with their demands. Again, because of their putative expertise in the field of their work they tend to monopolize not just the job but all accepted opinion on who should do the job, what it takes to do it, and how well it is being done. In principle, it would clearly be to the citizen consumer's advantage to have an informed, tough purchasing agent driving the best bargain possible for public goods of an amount, quality, kind, and mix his best judgment told him were in the interests of the people of his municipal corporation. Though such bargaining could scarcely be to the liking of educators, police, firemen, doctors, welfare workers, and other professionals and their unions, it might just suit the general public.

In principle, this Lakewood Plan approach should have taught us a lot. The municipal comparison shopping should have given us at least some of the performance yardsticks Ridley and Simon sought long ago and finally despaired of producing. Though much water has gone under the bridge since their effort, progress in evaluating municipal performance has not advanced far beyond where they left it. In a recent volume of essays on the quality of urban life, edited by Schmandt and Bloomberg, not one essay had a useful indicator measuring changes in some dimension of quality or relating such change to an observable characteristic of local government.[2] Even more recently, in a volume on metropolitan finance edited by Patrick Crecine of Michigan, Meltsner, and Wildavsky urged that we leave municipal budgeting alone and not try to install P.P.B.S. on the interesting ground that the impoverished city of Oakland, California, on which they based their study, was too poor to afford the analytical talent needed to determine whether it was getting its money's worth for its expenditures.[3] One can only suppose that the authors' pessimism is about the cost effectiveness of existing analytical capacity to determine whether a city is getting its money's worth, not that such information would not be worth having if attainable at a cost within reason.

But something that logically ought to work will only work in practice if there is sufficient isomorphism between the theory and its logic and the relevant variables that in reality control the phenomenon the theory is designed to explain. It seems hard to believe that Lakewood-type municipal purchasing agents would not on balance do far more good than harm. What does come through is that one of the assumptions of the classical economists' theory of the market—perfect information among buyers and sellers—is a bit far fetched. Public-choice theorists have gotten beyond this assumption, but they may not have found a way to get around it. The assumptions of rationality and rational self-interest are necessary to produce logically entailed and hence predictable results, but those properties with which abstract actors may be endowed for theory-building must not be confused with the properties of human actors that they may quite imperfectly reflect.

Thus, the purchase of patent medicine is a problem for the economist. The patent medicine is a part of the gross national product. The manufacturer profits. The workers are paid. The consumers seem satisfied and buy more. Why is it not an economic good rather than a waste of resources? Some such problem is also present in public goods, many of which may themselves be more or less expensive patent medicines. Like patent medicines such value as they have derives from their placebo effect. (Perhaps this latter is not something to be sniffed at, at least if its costs are not prohibitive.)

Even if there are reasons to doubt that differences in the quantity and quality of services provided by different suburbs can account for desired and ascribed differences in the efficacity of their public goods, the belief in the reality of these differences is generally acted on. And since it is, this has consequences in the real world quite apart from the validity of the assumptions on which the belief is based.

Take the case of education. If Ivar Berg is right, the credentials are what count. If the expensive suburban school is accorded the credentials by the educational establishment, it matters little what Berg or Coleman has to say about the rationality of this belief. The education establishment has the keys to educational approbation and the ultimate indication of it, entrance to the most prestigious academic institutions. Since most of the world, save Comrade Mao, moves in an increasingly Mandarin-type meritocracy, this is the gateway to the opportunity structure of the society, and the educators are the gatekeepers. Now, it is the function of the suburb not only to segregate access to the consumption of public goods, which might be supportable, but to segregate access to the opportunity structure by ensuring the differential availability of the opportunity for education. And by ensuring educational differences it creates the credentialized means for justifying the difference in access. Ultimately, by providing differential credentials resting on putative differences in educational achievement, the system legitimates, in terms of the society's achievement norm, the ensuing differences in status and income that differences in educational credentials entail.

In our type of society, perhaps the best estate that a middle-class family can give its offspring is a good suburban education leading to entrance to a good college and thence to a good job. The achieving father of an under-achieving son can try to head off his downward mobile fate by securing for him the benefits of a good suburban school and the good influences it provides. (The working-class equivalent is apprentice training and entrance to the union and trade. Nepotism, long known in the English professions, has its attractions for members of the stable working class.)

The charmed circle of the embryonic status structure of our public goods society runs from housing to education, from education to jobs and matrimony, from these to income, and from income back to housing again, completing the circle. Seen from this perspective, the metropolitan public goods market appears less as an ingenious device to satisfy differing tastes in public goods than as a means of avoiding the equality norms of the society in one of their most fundamental applications, the equality of educational opportunity. Though there is concern about physical matters, such as highways, sewage, water supply, transportation, and the more recently seen ills of pollution, the major issue in the functioning of the metropolitan public goods market revolves around the seemingly blatant inequalities of its distribution of the goods of health, education, and welfare. As Robert Wood remarks,[4] it segregates needs from resources.

Toronto Metro, the most successful metropolitan government on the continent, was doubtless originally conceived mainly to deal with a desperate backlog of problems of water supply, sewage, highways, and school construction, and these were the stock in trade of its George Washington, Frederic Gardiner. But once under way, it has moved seemingly inexorably toward the equalization of such public goods as education.

In the process, it radically reduced the number of its original constituent units. When Mr. H. Carl Goldenberg, a one-man Royal Commission, was appointed in 1963 to look into Toronto Metro's ten-year performance, he concluded that the observed disparities in public services standards and the variations in tax burdens necessary to support a given standard of service were far too great. Accordingly, he recommended consolidation of the thirteen municipalities into four cities to reduce these inequities. The Ontario parliament passed an act consolidating the thirteen municipalities into six boroughs. The logic of equal services to ensure the equality of equal citizens is difficult to avoid once the citizens are under one local government tent such as Toronto Metro.

In a paper given at Kansas City in 1965, Harold Kaplan remarked,

Thanks to Metro, critical service shortages in the suburban areas have been alleviated. The Metro system has achieved much less in the fields of housing, welfare and downtown redevelopment. The City of Toronto has been left to meet its most difficult problems on its own. Metro, moreover, has not succeeded in equalizing either the quantity or quality of services from one municipality to another and has not equalized the municipal tax rates.[5]

Perhaps because the deficiencies became apparent the Goldenberg report eventuated, and action to equalize services and pool fiscal capabilities ensued. W. J. McCordic, director and secretary-treasurer of the Metropolitan Toronto school board, believes that the two-tier plan that has pooled the resources of the area and permitted over-all budgeting and planning with considerable flexibility and autonomy of administration by the school boards of Metro's constituents has "demonstrated that consolidation of finance can lead toward equality of educational opportunity, without necessitating the surrender of significant autonomy by existing local units." He feels that "there is no obvious reason why a similar formula might not be equally successful elsewhere."[6]

But McCordic is well aware of some of the obvious reasons why this formula is difficult to apply in the United States. He recalls that in 1965 he gave a progress report on the Toronto experiment to a group of students at the London School of Economics.

The American participants listened in disbelief that a reorganization of local government of this magnitude could have been imposed, as it were, from above. With a passion that confirmed their own strong support for the principle, they stated that such a development would be impossible in the United States, since it could only be achieved with the consent of the governed.

American experience, as he points out, bears out the students' contention. But he finds other reasons

even more serious and fundamental than this that inhibit major reform of municipal government: two of them are race and poverty. Instinctively middle class suburban communities, which have proliferated throughout the length and breadth of the land, fight to remain insulated from involvement with nearby ghettos or slums. The spill-over effect once the barrier of a municipal boundary has been removed leads quickly to acute housing, welfare and school problems. Despite the national commitment to fight against discrimination, to recognize the right of racial minorities, and to help the economically deprived, the struggle at the local level continues. The upper middle class in particular are determined to remain aloof from these issues by any constitutional means available to them, particularly insofar as their public schools are concerned.[7]

There is some evidence of bussing blacks to suburban schools around Boston and elsewhere that would soften this comment though not change its force. And voting statistics on open-occupancy ordinances in Kansas City and other cities show a tendency for upper-income wards and blacks to combine. Certainly, blue-collar whites are equally if not more adamant on the issue.

It might seem somewhat schizophrenic that through one public-choice mechanism, the national or state government, we choose one set of public goods or state one set of intentions and through another mechanism, our local governments, choose a differing and even incompatible set of public goods with unstated but quite conflicting intentions. It is not, however, uncommon in human affairs for men to want their cake and to eat it too, to pray on Sunday for the grace to love their neighbor and then on Monday seek to keep him as far away as possible. The mechanisms of public choice, different agencies of government, are de-

signed to relate to the choice of different goods. As Gail
Cook points out,

The satisfaction of alternative preferences for local goods (goods
having benefits and costs which are restricted to the municipality) is in some cases facilitated by decentralized decision-making
through fragmented units while provision of area-wide goods
(goods having benefits and costs which extend throughout the
metropolitan area) requires decision-making at the metropolitan
level.

The greater the number of local units there are to produce
local public goods and the more homogeneous their clientele, the better people's choices can be served. But for
area-wide goods, transport systems, regional planning, and
the like the capacity to choose "varies inversely with the
number of political units, the source of the spill over, its
potential subjection to the price system and other determi-
nants." These polar forms of public choice are mechanisms
for exercising existing preferences for public goods. As Professor Cook points out,

An additional complication is introduced if the public sector is
viewed as a means of shaping social change. Then, for example,
the means of permitting expression of alternative demands for
public services (homogeneous political units) is in conflict with
the means of achieving children's school exposure to those of
dissimilar backgrounds (heterogeneous political units). Such inconsistent goals demand compromise solutions.[8]

But, of course, one of the things we wish to bring about in
a changing world is a functional adaptation to change.
However, how to accomplish this without running the risk
to our own desirable state presents problems for us and for
equilibrium analysis.

In effect, we desire two goods or one good that may be
satisfied in two ways, ways that are in conflict and ways
that involve different units of government in their pursuit.
We wish to reduce poverty and racial discrimination, per-

haps because by doing so we believe our own safety, amenities, and enjoyment would be enhanced. The national and state governments are regarded as the appropriate units through which to realize this state of affairs. In their effort to accomplish these ends, these units come into conflict with an alternative strategy pursued through local governments to solve our problem of personal security, amenities, and enjoyment through achieving our physical separation from the problems of race and poverty and their seeming attendant ills of crime, blight, squalor, and dependency. Physical and personal segregation from the problems was for a long time the strategy of the older city with its good neighborhoods, good schools, and policing. The impossibility of maintaining that strategy and the possibilities of the automobile and the truck have led to the replication of the older city on a metropolitan scale but with governments to defend its new neighborhoods, political walls to be policed and without a common government, short of the state, to press the claims of inhabitants who are not citizens to receive equal treatment.

The older city was heterogeneous, mixing classes, races, faiths, conditions, and occupations in a single political unit. However weak, there was a bond of common citizenship among its inhabitants. Though lacking the ultimate importance of the objects of the Greek city-state, the older city had, and has, high concerns—poverty and prosperity, class, religious and racial accommodation. It can mobilize men and materials in major amounts; its affairs by no stretch of the imagination can be considered trivial. It is a thing apart from what Scott Greer called the "toy governments of suburbia" or Robert Wood the "suburban miniature." Tocqueville, who is the major theorist of our local government, said, "The New Englander is attached to his township not so much because he was born in it, but because it is a free and strong community, of which he is a

member, and which deserves the care spent in managing
it. . . . [W]ithout power and independence, a town may
contain good subjects, but it can contain no active
citizens." [9] Tocqueville suggests another element of public
choice than that usually conceived by the economist as a
public good, namely, the opportunity to act as a significant
citizen rather than merely to be satisfied as a consumer.

The role of the citizen of Lakewood, comfortable in his
homogenized country club of like-minded fellows with little to do locally but consider the effectiveness of his pur-
chasing-agency government, contrasts with the harried citizen of the older heterogeneous city on the forefront and
firing line of race relations, hard-core unemployment,
crime, urban blight, and most other great issues of society.
Few, of course, may see the heterogeneous city as a challenge and the place where the issues must be met if they
are to be met. But the possibility of playing a role in such
a meaningful theater of action is itself one of the values of
a democratic society. Perhaps as much a value as the possibility of enjoying a wilderness or a Grand Canyon, and
one, it may be, that some must find attractive if the issues
of the society are to be resolved. It would be to our greatest advantage if we knew whether the heterogeneous older
city or the increasingly homogenized set of interacting
governmental units of the metropolitan public goods market provides the most powerful and beneficent logic for
resolving our critical problems.

Seemingly, we ought to be able to compare, along
agreed-on critical and important dimensions, the performance of governments and systems of government such as
Los Angeles County, Miami Metro, and New York City
and to evaluate the comparative cost effectiveness of their
performances. We do not have the data to make the com-
parisons. For the most part we are limited to a priori reasoning, the esthetics of organizational design and senti-

ment. One supposes that the condition of blacks in the all black suburb of Kinloch should be worse, given their inferior per capita resources, than is the condition of their fellows in Saint Louis. Certainly despite the wealth of Saint Louis County, the county is a far poorer mechanism of redistribution of resources than the city. Though it has been suggested that Kinloch's schools should be closed since they are black and segregated and their resources are substandard, it is not clear that their pupils are markedly worse off because of these deficiencies than the pupils in comparable schools in the city. Whether bussing in the county would be more feasible and productive of better results than in the city is unknown. In any event, till James Coleman's findings are reckoned with we do not know that altering the resource base would favorably alter the performance or, indeed, whether altering the academic performance would alter the life chances of the students.

The little that we do know about Kinloch is that its public housing is decent, well kept, and light years away from the City of Saint Louis's notorious Pruitt-Igoe. What this proves and what accounts for the difference remains to be discovered. We do know that people leave the city and go to Kinloch; few return. It is cheaper and allegedly safer. But when blacks have a choice they go to University City, a middle-class downward mobile suburb of Saint Louis with a reputedly good school system, professional police, and first-class city government. Presumably the blacks who go to University City want what the whites who left the city before them wanted, namely, security, housing, and schools. If white flight from University City substantially exceeds white willingness to stay in or come to the community, there is but one way for its housing to go, down. There simply are not enough middle-class and stable working-class blacks with the incomes to maintain the property values. Empty houses, vandalized houses, and ultimately

48

overoccupied and downward mobile housing use must follow the radical change in the income characteristics of the occupants. This process clearly homogenizes the suburb to a single use, and in that sense creates greater choice. Indeed for low-income blacks it is perhaps the most effective way to expand the limited range of their housing choices. Bernard Frieden of M.I.T. has maintained [10] that one of the worst features of the American system of supplying housing by hand-me-down is its cost in complete neighborhood turnover.

This process is likely to result not only in the rapid deterioration of the housing stock but in the deterioration of the community's stored-up stock of human capital. If it has had good schools, good police, and a professionally manned government, those not locked in by civil service and retirement are likely, after a brief struggle, to leave. The atmosphere of such a community creates a general climate of disinvestment. Those concerns such as General Electric and Tow-Motor in East Cleveland, for example, must consider whether if they stay they will only represent a fat and lonely tax target in an extension of a central-city ghetto without the support of other businesses like themselves. Under such conditions of downward mobility the suburb has all the problems of the city without its assets. The limited capacity of many if not all homogenized suburbs to maintain themselves may be one of the most serious objections to them. In most of the tract subdivisions of suburbia there are neither the resources nor the commitment to pursue a policy of community conservation and stabilization. It is easier after a brief flurry to cut and run than to risk one's effort and capital in a struggle whose issue must seem dubious.

The point that Toronto Metro has moved to is six strong boroughs with a second-tier overhead government to deal with area-wide functions and to pool the metropolitan areas' resources in such a way as to make possible reasonable service standards without excessive tax burdens. Six boroughs represent a large diminution of choice compared to the rich variety of governmental units in most American metropolitan areas. Yet, the choice to have six boroughs represents, itself, a kind of choice, and a choice that needs to be judged by whether the new public-choice mechanism it sets up has measurably desirable results in the lives of the people it serves. Unfortunately, few architects of governmental change will specify the measurable observable improvements their innovations are guaranteed to entail. The American tradition of municipal reform in advocating the city manager plan and the model charter claimed the virtues of economy and efficiency for its brain children. In the event, they were embarrassed to find that the new governments spent more money than the old. Of course, they could still claim, and did, that they spent it more economically and efficiently. The Goldenberg report justifies its recommendation for the reform of Toronto Metro in terms of the need for equal service standards throughout the area and not at the price of any undue tax burden on the less affluent. The equalization of service standards, the presumed needs, and their relation to available resources is the most common argument for some pooling of fiscal capabilities and for imposition and support of common service levels throughout metropolitan areas.

But the cry for equal levels of service standards, though made in the hallowed name of equality, says nothing about the effect of the observance of the standards on people. It is readily understandable that policemen, firemen, teachers, and other functionaries should press for equal rates of pay, working conditions, and perhaps equipment and whatnot throughout a metropolitan area and do so in the name of standards. It is less clear just what this equalization has to do with the well-being of various groups among the metro-

politan population. The problem is much like that of building codes and performance standards. The building trades
and material suppliers are interested in legislating a building code that will protect the materials, the processes, and
interests of skill groups. This is done in the name of protecting the public, but is actually for the protection of
those who serve the public. If the performance characteristics of what is desired could be specified and its attainment tested, experimentation in new, cheaper, and better
ways of producing products the public desires could be
both permitted and encouraged. We have a fair idea from
the construction industry what minimum or desirable standards are in practice likely to be. Educators are not all
that different from the construction trades and are as balky
about substituting performance standards for their code requirements. Hutchins at Chicago made a valiant effort to
insist that if students could pass the examinations they
should be credited with having the knowledge no matter
how they got it. Clearly, it would be a revolutionary undertaking to set up performance standards for a unit of
local government and then accept its meeting these standards, no matter how.

Conceivably, an Amish one-room school with an uncerti-
fied high school girl as teacher might achieve as much, or
more, in giving its pupils the basic skills as a whole expensive school complex with all the standard equipment. By
conventional standards, the achieving Amish school would
be substandard, not the underachieving conventional
school system. A Black Muslim church in its neighborhood
might do as well as the Amish in theirs. Further, a Black
Muslim church might solve its members' and its neighborhoods' safety problem and make great inroads in its health
and welfare problems as well. Colonel Sanders, the chairman of the Saint Louis Police Board, testifying before the
hearings of the Democratic Platform Committee, told them,

"Basically the neighborhood has to police itself." [11] This suggests that there are do-it-yourself possibilities in government as well as a politics of purchased solutions. But to do it oneself rather than buy the product, an unusual degree of involvement of the citizens is required. They must be producers as well as consumers of public goods. To get them to do it themselves, a symbolic wall of a church, an ethnic or racial sense of identity, commitment, and difference that sets the members apart as something different from the normal free-floating factors of production and consumption of our market society is required.

Some such possibilities of innovative activity in the production of public goods are seen by public-choice theorists and account for their concern that a way be left open for intergovernmental competition in providing alternative vehicles for meeting the needs of people and their desires as well. The huge city faces the problem of activating its neighborhoods, however much its administrators may dread having the people in their hair. School boards naturally desire supportive and complacent P.T.A.'s, but have to recognize that parental apathy and unconcern with the school and their children is a costly drag on the educational effort. Police realize that, as Colonel Sanders recognized, in the end the neighborhoods must police themselves. The police are most effective when they are neighborhood agents in the maintenance of a law and order that the neighborhoods recognize as their own. The disintegration of the older neighborhoods with their normative structures and local systems of social control has placed an enormous dead weight on the city. The neighborhoods were the cellular structures of the city. They were places where, in Mayor Lindsay's sense, people did give a damn because they felt their care had a meaning. The bureaucratized state of dependency and mere consumership of public goods takes its revenge in the failure to give a damn, the lack of local structure through which to be able effectively to give a damn, and the reduction of citizenship to voting with one's feet.

It is not surprising in view of the problems of the big city, such as New York, itself a prime example of the creation of a metropolitan government in an earlier era, that many people should be wary of turning the metropolitan area into one big city. Even the Committee for Economic Development, once enamored of making big ones out of small ones, has receded to a federalist position. Most academics who feel the need for a layer of government between existing local governments in metropolitan areas and the states take the federalist posture, preferring a two-tier approach that would leave a measure of autonomy to existing local governments, though possibly with some consolidation among them, to seeking total amalgamation into a single unitary government. This position is taken for reasons of conviction and expediency. There is recognition of the real desirability of providing some reasonable measure of variety in the packages of public goods available in metropolitan areas and the need for this variety in order to promote citizen involvement in the lower units of local government. It is recognized as well that, given the attachment of people to their existing units of local government, there is far more chance of acquiescence in a change that would modify their powers by adding a metropolitan government to them than one that would replace them entirely.

Experience with metropolitan reform in the United States indicates that it is unlikely to come from below. Wherever the attempts have been made through local action with referenda, entrenched interests in the local status quo, folk conservatism, fear of higher taxes, and the unknown and growing concern among blacks that metropolitan reform would, in fact, if not in intent, serve to dilute their influence and possible control over central cities and older suburbs, have proved stubbornly resistant to change. Such success as metropolitan reform has had in the United States has been largely confined to the South, where the home-rule tradition is weak and a deferential democracy similar to Canada's still obtains. The persistent pressure for metropolitan reform comes from minor elements in the population, the intellectuals of local government, central-city officials, the metropolitan press, chambers of commerce of central cities, downtown stores and banks tied to their central cities, these and some elements of federal officialdom and Congress. These elements for a variety of reasons interest themselves in metropolitan reform, but more as a matter of program material for a civic project than as a matter of powerfully felt vital self-interest. Though the elements are prominent, vocal, articulate, and capable of commanding attention, they lack widespread popular support.

Metropolitan planning and councils of governments in metropolitan areas are developments that have occurred largely because the federal government has been willing to pay the fiddler. Should federal subvention cease with a withdrawal to unconditioned grants to the states (revenue-sharing) the continuance of these developments will depend on the interest of the states. It may be that in some places, such as the San Francisco Bay Area, the Association of Bay Area Governments, already in being in state law and with significant functions of its own, will continue even without federal funding. The jealousy of Bay Area officials of Sacramento and the proven utility of the new institution should ensure its continued life. Elsewhere the councils of governments are growing from forums of government officials, local United Nations, and staffs to make such studies as other governments and sources are willing to fund them to do to accepted instrumentalities of an emergent metropolitan community that sees these institutions as needed and useful instrumentalities for dealing with common problems. Thus far, the groping attempts to give governmental recognition to the social and economic unity of metropolitan areas have come more from senior government, federal and state, than local. The Ford Foundation and departments of the U.S. government have shown more dollar interest in pioneering these developments than anyone else.

The country has undergone major changes since independence and the framing of the Constitution, but these changes have received little recognition in our political theory, and except for some expediential tinkering, not much has occurred in the formal reshaping of our institutions. In the eyes of Jefferson, though perhaps not those of the presidential Jefferson, man's first loyalty was to himself and family, then to his town, then his state, and at long last to the federal union. The fundamental political institutions of the country in the beginning were the states, the successors after the Revolution to the sovereignty of England. The Constitution was an expediential contrivance of the states to improve over the Articles of Confederation for certain area-wide purposes, notably common defense, foreign affairs, currency, interstate commerce, and the western lands. With the Civil War what many thought was a confederation became in fact a nation in which the Union clearly emerged, in any ultimate contest, supreme. With the forming of new states, mass migration at home and from abroad, loyalties that had centered on states and state government became fixed on the Union and the national government. Where once had been a confederation of states a nation had emerged.

But we did our best to avoid recognizing this fact. We were supposedly an indestructible union of indestructible states; only in case of conflict the Supreme Court would decide, and the umpire played on the national team. Little thought was given after the Civil War to what institutional changes were needed to recognize the emergent fact of nationality. In the nightwatchman state of laissez-faire capitalism, the national government had few domestic duties. The federal government did violate the pure doctrine of laissez-faire in a policy of protectionism and public private-works promotion such as the railways. And where the chief constituency lay there never was a constitutional scruple about federal activity. Washington has never shown a bad conscience about helping farmers, at least some of them, and even creating elaborate quasilocal governments in the process. Marble-cake rather than layer-cake federalism, as Joseph McLean and Morton Grodzin have insisted, has been the rule, not just recently but from the beginning. But our preponderant ideology, the way people liked to look at themselves and their government, has been the norm of laissez-faire and free private enterprise.

What characterized the earlier federal intervention was its relation to agriculture, public works, and rural rather than urban areas. The cities, when they were thought of, were the province of the states save when the federal troops were needed to quell strikes. The Great Depression brought to a head the slowly maturing forces of change. By then the country had become a predominantly urban and industrial nation, even though the preferred perspective in Washington and even more in state governments was one of the rural and agricultural past. The Depression showed that in a crunch neither local governments nor states were fiscally strong enough to withstand its ravages. Sooner or later the national government as the one institution with the fiscal strength had to bail them out. The collapse of the states occasioned for a time some serious thought about their restructure. Their wide disparities in population and resources made them seem hopelessly unfit to provide a standard array of services in the emerging urban industrial society. The criticism of them leveled at that time is oddly reminiscent of the Goldenberg report on Toronto Metro. But all attempts at finding some set of overlay maps delimiting problem areas, population, and resources that would produce a better natural fit than the existing states proved unpersuasive. With the return of a modicum of prosperity, enthusiasm for restructuring the states waned; they remained unreformed and going concerns.

But if the states were unreformed, the orientation of the national government and its relation to the cities was profoundly changed. From the nightwatchman state of nineteenth-century laissez-faire, with occasional backsliding into promotionalism and a heretical commitment to tariffs and protection, the federal government moved into the twentieth-century mainstream of the welfare state. It did so with a constitutional bad conscience and only after a bitter struggle with a Supreme Court that in Justice Holmes's quip sought to enact Herbert Spencer's social statics. It was, perhaps, a misfortune that the national government had to find its way to the assistance of its urban constituency through the spending power. The so-called elastic clause of the Constitution, permitting the federal government to spend money for the general welfare, made it possible to bribe and blackmail the states to use their police powers in fashions the national government found desirable but beyond the strict scope of its own constitutional authority. In practice, this denied to the national government its own system of local government and required it to pursue its policies through officials who might prefer to march, and actually in fact to march to a different drum.

As the national government moved in the direction of becoming a welfare state in an urban industrial rather than rural and agricultural setting, it was in the anomalous position of lacking a delivery system of its own. In the field of agriculture the federal government had assisted in the development of a complex interacting system of land-grant colleges, agricultural extension, county agents, Farm Bureau federation, and a varying array of state and county agencies. This complex with the county agent, the Farm Bureau, extension, and the land-grant college had proved immensely successful in increasing the productivity of American agriculture. On the side of welfare, however, except for the welfare of the affluent farmers and their allies of the Farm Bureau federation, it had done little if anything to help small farmers, sharecroppers, farm laborers. The majority of those in agriculture and the country's consuming public were not even recognized as a party at interest. Unlike its operation in the agricultural field, for the most part the federal government proceeded through grants to the states and through state agencies that had the constitutional power to perform the desired function. Without a common focus a varied assortment of special programs developed lacking any coordination or relation among them. In some cases, such as housing, the states were largely bypassed entirely. Still later, when federal disenchantment set in, the President's Committee on Juvenile Delinquency and its successor, the Office of Economic Opportunity, sought to bypass to an important degree both state and local bureaucracies.

The proliferation of federal government grant programs has become something of a scandal. For some time it has been the object of attack by governors who found it eroding their independence of action and budgetary control. The Advisory Commission on Intergovernmental Relations has documented its growth. It is a piecemeal and patchwork edifice without architect or design, representing the results of coalitions and pressures, adding this and that program to the structure. Yet when President Eisenhower sought to return to the states programs that the federal government had arrogated to itself he found but a couple that could be agreed on as ripe for return, and even on these he could get no action. What seemed and seems most amiss about the whole business is its lack of any over-all order or concerted design. Like Topsy, it has just grown. But unlike Topsy, its consequences are more than comical. The grants program the states in ways they frequently would not choose. Who, if he can get 90 per cent money from the federal government for 10 per cent of his own and knows the expedience of putting men and contractors to work, will spend his dollars in areas other than highways, blessed with less potent multipliers or none at all?

It is not just the complex maze of federal grants, requiring special experts and Washington offices for states and cities as well as corporations, that causes concern but the growing realization that this historic accumulation takes on a life of its own. No one knows whether in its interactive entirety it is good or bad, and most suspect that it is enormously wasteful. Given the incremental budgetary process that Wildavsky pictures in Washington, once a program is in, its share of the governmental market gets reviewed, not its cost effectiveness and least of all its relatedness to a well-considered, or even considered, general program. In addition to the grant programs, there are the programs of line departments such as Housing and Urban Development (H.U.D.), Health, Education and Welfare, the Department of Transportation, and the Pentagon. Much time has passed since Connery and Leach documented the unintended and conflicting impacts of the federal government on the cities. Eisenhower, in recognition, gave Bob Merriam the job of refereeing the battle. Neither then nor since, through the convenor order of H.U.D. by which President Johnson sought to have the housing agency take the lead in bringing a common sense to the varied federal undertakings in and around the cities, has the White House or the Congress been able to produce program coordination of the federal impact.

The high tide of the federal effort was probably the proposal for a model cities expediter in the model cities legislation. The expediter, originally expected by some to have assistant secretary rank, would have had the field job of pooling the various federal programs being put in the common pot of the model city area. The expediter had promise of developing into H.U.D.'s and the President's man in the metropolitan areas. Before the exigencies of the Vietnam War occasioned a strategic retreat from the Great Society, H.U.D. appeared to be moving toward attaining the role of a ministry of metropolitan government in the national welfare state that seemed to be emerging. The Department of Agriculture, hard up for farmers and casting about for new business, put in its bid to become the nation's ministry of rural government, and the Department of Interior, not to be left out entirely, turned its attention east in search of business in recreation and water resources. For a time at least these federal initiatives were given a severe check by the Vietnam War, inflation, fiscal stringency, and the election of a Republican president committed to the Eisenhower goals of returning power to the states by revenue-sharing. With the drive toward revenue-sharing, it seemed possible that even the federal initiative for metropolitan planning and councils of governments might lose its force unless the states showed more interest in these activities than they had in the past.

In the pre-Nixon period it seemed as if an activist national government accepting the role of a welfare state would see in the nation's metropolises the appropriate population divisions for coordination of its previously merely coexistent and often conflicting programs. The advantage to the national government in using such areas as a program focus could be enormous. Coordination cannot exist meaningfully for its own sake. If it is to be more than an empty ritual in Washington or some regional center, coordination needs must be for some specifiable population's sake. This is why in a public-choice sense it might make sense for the national government to choose the metropolises, where the overwhelming majority of its constituency lives and works, as targets for its local delivery system, in effect its system of local government. A main advantage of the metropolitan areas is their nonhomogeneity, their diversity, which makes them representative samples of the people and problems of the country. Further, as interacting systems, taking them whole makes possible and imperative consideration of the interacting nature of federal programs, federally supported programs, and other state and local programs. The total outcome of these programs on the important aspects of the city dwellers' lives—housing, health, income, jobs, education, recreation, and the like—would be the criterion for evaluation of the cost effectiveness and human worth of government programs. In this fashion the public-choice mechanism can be both evaluated in its practice and, hopefully, improved.

In a recent speech Sol Linowitz, former board chairman of Xerox and presently chairman of the Urban Coalition, points out that

Over the last twenty years, some 80% of the new jobs created in the nation's largest metropolitan areas have been in the suburbs. Most of these new jobs are unskilled or semi-skilled—precisely the kind of jobs that central-city blacks or low income whites could fill, if they could find some feasible ways of getting between home and job. They cannot, however, afford to commute by private transportation; and under the best of circumstances, public transportation is too costly or too time-consuming or both. . . . The flight of industry into the suburbs is often explained on economic grounds. Far more difficult to explain is the failure of industry to enable its workers to follow them.

This blindness and unwillingness to use industry's clout on behalf of opening up the suburbs to permit the low-income residents of the city to follow their jobs to the suburbs is a major cause of misery and potential violence. "Morally and economically," Linowitz urges, "the effort to match workers and jobs makes as good sense for business as it does for society." [12] The mismatch of jobs and residence of low and unskilled categories of workers may be another fruit of a process of homogenization rather than heterogenization of public goods. If the goal is to employ the unemployed and the underemployed, homogenization of industry to areas of the suburbs where their previous and potential employees cannot follow is a disaster. If, on the other hand, the goal is to escape this population and seek a quite different labor force, it makes abundant sense. The quandary of the federal and other governments is shown in the celebrated Black Jack case, where a Saint Louis suburb incorporated in order to zone out a project of low- and middle-income housing.[13]

The mismatch of jobs and housing is one example of the results of ways in which a particular public-choice mechanism can homogenize in such fashion as to permit choices whose consequences are badly mixed. The tax-haven suburb for industry and the middle-class and even wholly stable working-class suburb may, via the results of choosing them, amount to the choice of the causes of educational failure, unemployment, underemployment, dependency, and crime. Unfortunately, a tested theory linking these results to homogenization does not exist. The problem of employment is clear enough, and it spells out fairly clearly the consequences of failing to make choices that adequately relate housing, transportation, and jobs. If the Coleman report stands up, there would seem reason to examine carefully the results of class segregation on education and the motivation and aspirations of children. Coleman found that one of the main factors affecting children's success lay in their belief in the degree to which their own actions could affect their fate. The belief in one's own causal efficacy was much higher in a middle-class milieu. This argues that a policy of seeking to distribute rather than homogenize the poor would be a rational public choice if one's goal was to increase the likelihood of the latter's children being more achievement-oriented. Such a choice would not deny that an Amish community, a Black Muslim or an evangelical church, might not be able under homogenized conditions of low income to achieve similar motivations. It would in all likelihood, however, regard these special communities as scarce factors with a low and limited capacity for generalization. Whether this latter is the case is an interesting and important question that bears on the range of real options through which desired levels of education and achievement motivation can be obtained.

It seems not wholly impossible to plan a metropolitan area to achieve the goals of heterogeneity rather than the present homogenizing drift. The Dayton Plan includes twenty-nine Ohio municipalities and five counties in the Dayton, Ohio, area which approved a housing dispersal plan in September 1970. The white suburbs ringing the central city agreed to provide shares of 14,000 units of low- and moderate-income housing expected to be built in the next four years. A regional housing plan such as this needs to be matched by a regional manpower plan. Presumably the administration's 1969 manpower bill intended to bring about such a plan and its implementation. Achieving the manpower objectives in all likelihood would be found to involve metropolitan transportation planning and metropolitan educational planning, at least in the fields of vocational and technical education and quite possibly, if educational resources were to be effectively tailored to local manpower requirements, other areas of education as well.

THE UNWALLED CITY

The inflationary consequences of too heavy a reliance on macro-Keynesian policies to deal with what the economists call the rigidities of the labor market exact too heavy a price. It is even doubtful that paying the price would achieve the desired result. The inflation attendant on the Vietnam War certainly has not. More expressly designed measures, such as Swedish manpower planning, seem in order if a public policy to promote employability is to be successful. Such a policy runs head on into some of the rigidities of the labor market attributable to the choice of public goods homogenization.

The Nixon administration has turned to the states, a move in the Eisenhower tradition and more in line with Republican ideological commitments than the drive toward a direct federal relation with local governments or their inhabitants. The change in direction was already heralded by the Heller Pechman plan, which fell foul of Vietnam stringencies. The more extreme tendencies of the Office of Economic Opportunity and its C.A.P.'s to bypass the power structure of states and cities had been curbed before Nixon's arrival on the Washington scene. Moynihan wrote an epitaph for maximum feasible participation of the poor in his comment on maximum feasible misunderstanding.[14] The Nixon approach, in theory at least, elected to right the balance among the mechanisms of public choice by a resort to "creative federalism," principally, it would appear, through revenue-sharing. The large number of special empires created by federal grant programs allying bureaucracies in Washington, the states and the local scene would no longer be a law unto themselves. By replacing grant programs with general-purpose grants, states and governors would no longer find their hands tied. And if one is seeking a place to make sense of a multitude of programs in terms of their effects on a defined population, using the states is one way to do it. Further, there is nothing to stop states from decentralizing their activities to metropolitan areas and co-opting local governments into the common enterprise.

The states, as critics often point out, are the governmental agencies having the constitutional responsibility for local government and the cities which legally are their creations. In Canada, the provinces have taken vigorous action to rethink and redesign the pattern of local government. Canada, even more than the United States, has been urbanizing, suburbanizing, and metropolitanizing. According to Lionel D. Feldman and Michael D. Goldrick, "Geographers suggest that within two decades a majority of Canadians will reside in six cities, and principally in two, Montreal and Toronto." [15] Yoshiko Kasahara has shown that the metropolitan explosion in Canada was actually a suburban explosion.[16] Without the problem of race Canada's urban history has developed along lines much like the United States. The homogenization downward of the central cities with the departure of the affluent followed by the middle class and elements of the working class is similar. And cities such as Toronto have been subject to major migration flows from abroad paralleling in their magnitude the American migration to the cities from Puerto Rico and the South. Similar problems of central-city adjustment have ensued.

Though the Canadian provinces have been far more responsive to the needs of the cities and local government than the American states, their difficulties in handling a problem of national dimensions have been much the same. Feldman and Goldrick point out that in "the summer of 1968, the Treasurer of Ontario, Canada's richest province was quoted in the *Globe and Daily Mail* as saying that municipalities, recognizing the strictures on provincial budgets were looking to the federal government for direct aid." [17] These developments have caused Hans Blumenfeld, the famous planner, to remark, "As metropolitan regions become the home of an overwhelming majority of Canadians, their problems are bound to become more and more identical with those of Canada. To modify a famous—or infamous—quotation, 'What is good for the nation is good for its urban areas—and vice versa.' " [18] This is a fine rhetorical flourish, but it fails to deal with whether, in achieving what is good for the nation, which may well be what is good for its urban areas, that good is better pursued by using the provinces and the states as important parts of the complex mechanism of public choice. The argument has been twofold: (1) Provinces and states have been considered too deficient in revenue potential to deal with the problem. (2) In the United States at any rate, the states have been regarded, with some reason, as uninterested and incompetent and the federal government as constitutionally inappropriate, too remote, and bureaucratically ineffective.

Perhaps the most serious flaw in the Nixon administration's plan to activate a creative federalism that would rouse the states to their urban responsibilities is the powerful force of tradition in the states. The cities, especially the central cities, have a profound and justified suspicion of state governments. Long ago they sought home rule as a means of avoiding being kept in leading strings or, worse, being subjected to heavy charges imposed on them by special interests working through legislatures that responded to pressure when the city, not the state, was to bear the burden. Mayor Lindsay, in rhetorically seeking status for New York City as a state, has real grounds for his complaints in the willingness of the state legislature to up the city's costs without concern for where the money would come from. This history of adversary relations and neglect is difficult to forget. Nor has "one man, one vote" improved the lot of the city or older decaying suburbs. The enfran-

66

chisement of the suburban middle class and its proportionate representation in the legislature has increased the power of an electorate that in some things sees eye to eye with the cities but in many sides with the older rural-business alliance. Certainly its special breaks from the state government are unlikely to be foregone because of any sense of equity or comparative need. More important, the very amenities orientation that brought the suburban migration is likely to give its weight a force more in the direction of ecological issues and the enhancement of amenities than in that of a redistributive effort or even a concerted interest in pressing for effective state planning of human resource development.

Conceivably the states could serve as appropriate areas for manpower planning, human and natural resource development and management. With such a mission they could decentralize the state's administration to its metropolitan areas as principal subareas for both formulating and implementing the state's plans for its people. The decentralization of state administration might be one aspect of a serious attempt by state government to look at its local government structure and relate that structure to the public choices the people of the state wished to be able to make and to enable its constituent populations to make. With an over-all set of goals for the people of the state spelled out in health, income, jobs, housing, education, amenities, and the like, it becomes possible to test the desirability of particular local government mechanisms as devices appropriate for the suitable attainment of the goals the state might have in mind, including some reasonable variation in the mix of goals and degree of goal attainment as desired by subpopulations through their several local government choice mechanisms. To state this, however, is to see that if indeed there is some trend in this direction it is a highly uncertain one. Under conditions of financial stringency and without strong pressure from below, an unlikely occurrence, such a development will depend on federal pressure on the states.

In fact the major hope of the states in the Nixon program is the lightening of their burdens through revenue-sharing. A like hope exists with the cities, whose main concern is to make sure of a mandatory pass through that will ensure that they get their share of the federal money. The Heller-Pechman plan, which initiated the movement toward revenue-sharing, had quite other objects in view than alleviating the fiscal ills of states and cities. The original concern was with the so-called fiscal drag the adverse effect of which on the economy was feared once Vietnam was over and the predicted fiscal dividend ensued. Federal spending was supposed to lag behind federal revenues, just the reverse of the plight of the states. Accordingly, Heller and Pechman proposed to cure the fiscal mismatch of resources and needs by tying the states into the more elastic federal revenue structure. The fiscal dividend for state or federal programs has proved as evanescent, in the poetic words of Moynihan, as the mists of San Clemente, even though the President has striven manfully to redirect enough old program spending to give revenue-sharing some semblance of reality. Many state and local officials are vocal in their support of revenue-sharing not because the present magnitude of the funding is more than a token but because of the principle involved, and perhaps because the whole program makes it appear that state and city problems are money problems and even lack of federal money problems—a comforting out.

A Brookings Institution study [19] of federal income and expenditures makes it painfully clear that the Heller-Pechman concern with a fiscal drag was unwarranted. The fiscal dividend will be small for a year or two, and even when it gathers steam could readily be erased by an increase in social security benefits or a reduction in the payroll tax, its major source. Any one of the major federal programs, such as increase in health care, a realistic welfare level, or a major effort to improve the environment would pretty well wipe out any federal funds available to the states. Holding out the hope of a federal fiscal bail-out is likely to be counterproductive to states and cities by permitting the Micawber policy of hoping something will turn up to continue. As Lyle Fitch has remarked,[20] the federal fiscal dividend is probably already earmarked for the next round of public employee wage demands. The prospect of it may serve to postpone facing up to the painful problem of the inflation of government costs, the sagging productivity of the public sector and what to do about public employee power. The misfortune of the concentration on getting handouts from senior levels of government is that it leads to the avoidance of the question of whether at some level local economies do not have to be self-sustaining. Clearly, neither the nation nor the states can survive if all beneath them is in the red. They have no magic pitcher save the printing press, and the Vietnam inflation hangover should have taught us something.

It would be of considerable value to our thinking about appropriate government structures if we had a better understanding of the nature of local economies and the relation of government and governments to their functioning. From the point of all concerned it is a bad thing to have a set of dependent political poor relations existing on sufferance by handouts from other governments and levels of government. Such units of government are likely to become so many Indian reservations manned with keepers and sinking further and further into economic dependency. In cities and suburbs these reservations outside of or hangers-on of the mainstream economy are likely to combine welfare with crime, drug addiction, and an intergenerationally transmitted culture of poverty. A major consideration in looking at the public-choice mechanism of a system of intergovernmental relations is to examine the ways it allocates its human and material resources. The existence of large numbers of unemployed and underemployed, young and old, the failure to develop skills, inadequacy of transport to relate place of residence to jobs, the premature obsolescence of housing and business structures, the absence of healthy profit incentives that pay people to invest in rather than milk property—all these are criteria for evaluating the functioning of a local political economy.

At the present time neither nation, state, nor metropolitan planning area has set up books on the functioning of the metropolitan area. That many an older city and suburb, and some not that old, is subject to what seems the wasteful and premature decay of its physical plant seems abundantly clear. That a significant body of the people of the metropolitan area are unemployed and underemployed is likewise clear. How much of this is due to the present organization or lack of organization of the metropolitan area? Not all the unemployment and underemployment can be attributed to federal fiscal policy. Much of it preceded it. How much could be done by existing cities and towns in the metropolitan area acting alone or in concert? The decision costs, to use the public-choice term, are fairly high for the limited leadership pool that exists in the metropolitan area. Perhaps the various governments of the area could be gotten to achieve some self-conscious cooperation in recognition of their sharing a common labor market, a common housing market, in fact, a common economy. But precisely one of the virtues of the market of the classical economist was that the buyers and suppliers functioning in it could follow their selfish interests, controlled by the market cues of price and profit and loss without need or capacity to think about or do anything about the over-all outcomes of the market. These by the logic of the market were unintentionally but inevitably beneficent. Many of the results of the present interaction of the metropolitan public goods market seem questionably beneficent, at least for the lives of many. Such a market needs to be humanly controlled and structured to serve humane purposes.

3

The Uneconomic
Politics of the City

THE METROPOLITAN AREAS of the United States contain the bulk, soon the overwhelming bulk, of its population, talent, and material resources. Despite the seeming adequacy of their resources the mayors are everywhere hat in hand at the doorsteps of state and national capitols begging for funds and pleading poverty and dire necessity. At first sight this seems odd. The main sources of state and national wealth are themselves not wealthy and must beg back a pittance of the taxes they pay to state and national treasuries. How in the midst of an unprecedented national affluence can one account for urban penury? First one must admit that despite the general complaint many local governments have a more than adequate balance between resources and needs. But many, in increasing numbers, do not. As noted earlier there is no necessary correspondence between resources and needs among the cities and towns of metropolitan areas. Indeed in much of the country, the central cities and older suburbs, built up at an earlier date and now faced with both declining revenues from obsolescent real estate and the increasing costs of a low tax-paying and high service-need population, experience a widening gap between their declining resource base and mounting needs. As a whole, metropolitan areas are wealthy, but many of their constituent parts are impoverished.

The local, state, and national tax structures are of such a character that the local is least broadly based, least income elastic, and most regressive. It falls on many as an oppressively high sales tax on housing. For the renter, unlike the home owner, there is no income-tax offset. This results in a public-housing subsidy for those best able to bear the burden of taxation and the denial of the subsidy to those least able. The incidence of real estate taxation is such as to discourage property maintenance and improvement and to encourage a policy of milking the property. The burden of the tax is such as to make the large number of marginal property owners extremely sensitive to increases in the property tax and in consequence a formidable obstacle where referenda on tax rate and bonding are necessary. It is a curious feature of the American polity that space, the military, and foreign aid come out of the income tax and the preponderant social expenditures of local government must be met by the sales and real estate taxes. One might wonder what would happen to the military if they had to persuade state legislatures to raise the sales tax of local voters to up the millage.

Of all the aspects of the local tax structure perhaps the most crucial is its income inelasticity. When incomes go up and prices go up, national revenues go up a great deal, state revenues moderately, and local revenues sluggishly indeed. Yet it is, as Galbraith has pointed out,[1] at the local government level where the greatest needs of the society are met if they are met at all. Local politicians must constantly struggle to raise taxes, which are keenly and painfully felt, just to meet increases in prices and wages, let alone to provide increased services. At a time of rising prices, taxpayers, who are themselves hard pressed, find themselves asked to pay more taxes for poorer services. Under these circumstances it is not difficult to see why mayors of even well-off communities try to tap federal funds.

The states, though in better shape by far than the cities, are still largely without broadly based, adequately elastic sources of revenue. Their own fiscal problems account in part for their niggardly behavior toward their cities. In addition, of course, the rural and suburban bias has resulted time and again in aid formulae that discriminate against the cities, and especially, the central cities. There is good reason for mayors' fears of any federal revenue-sharing plan that would leave them at the mercy of the states; even so state oriented a body as the Advisory Commission on Intergovernmental Relations is sensitive to their concern. Reliance on the real property tax condemns the cities both to a losing race with rising prices and wages and to a zero-sum game whose stakes are the location of plums with high tax yields and low service costs or lemons with low tax yields and high service costs.

A major obstacle in the way of effective metropolitan planning and cooperation has been municipal dependence on the property tax. Attempts to achieve a pattern of land use for the metropolitan area that might most efficiently site industry, minimize utility costs, reduce the journey to work, and preserve open space have been frustrated by the fact that almost everybody wanted a revenue-producing industrial park, almost nobody wanted a nonrevenue-producing public park, and fewer still wanted revenue-consuming low-income or public housing. And given the nature of the municipal profit and loss account it is difficult for even the most socially conscious and enlightened city manager to play the game any other way. Local municipalities are prepared, if need be, to share with those who have more than they do, even on occasion with those in the same bracket, but they resist tenaciously any attempt to force them into an unfavorable marriage. Fiscal zoning, frequently with requirements as stiff as five-acre lots, is a standard device to ensure that redistribution of income by local government will be kept within narrow limits, at least for those who can afford residence in the right suburban tax havens.

Yet the logic of economic interest is sometimes ambiguous and pulls in opposite and conflicting directions. The businessmen of Hartford—that is, the more economically enlightened of the big businessmen and in particular their representatives in the local chamber of commerce—were recently faced with the stubborn fact that their businesses could only expand in the Hartford area if they could have more workers. And they could only have more workers if there was housing for them. But there was no more room for housing expansion in Hartford. So if business were to expand, something somewhere in the suburbs would have to give. This put the businessmen in a quandary: As businessmen seeking to expand they needed housing for their labor force; as suburbanites seeking to preserve their tax base and the class homogeneity of their residences they, like their neighbors, had every interest in limiting the membership of their political country clubs. Then there was the question of who if not all should be made to accept the burden of the necessary but unwanted workers. Had there been a Hunter-type elite in Hartford the agony might have been short and the decision swift. There was not. The suburbs were not opened. And perhaps business should not have expanded in the Hartford area anyway. The conflict of interest, the deadlock, was but the working of the unseen hand.

Even where businessmen see the importance of opening suburban land as a means of housing their employees, or when they identify with the central city and seek to reverse trends that make it the receptacle for the surrounding areas' unskilled, poor, aged, blacks, and otherwise discriminated against, they have rarely been able or sufficiently motivated to reverse the powerful logic that is built into the existing system and produces this result. The logic of an ecology of governments dependent on the property tax creates a beggar-my-neighbor policy of competitive behavior modified by only limited cooperation for the most limited and urgent needs or the most unthreatening objectives. The classical prisoner problem of economics is recognized by many in the ecology of governments. But the advantages of submerging local sovereignties are less tempting than are the psychic rewards of the status quo, at least, to the most highly involved actors whose desire to remain big frogs in small puddles is backed by the folk conservatism of their constituents and a powerful set of locally vested interests.

The ecology of local governments shows much the same tendency to exist and endure, in its less glamorous way, as that of ancient Greece. The classic method of overcoming divisions through the expansion of one of the contending units has been limited in much of the country by the intervention of the states. When Milwaukee, for example, sought to use its highly developed municipal water system as a bargaining lever to force annexation and break out of its suburban encirclement to open land and a share of the taxes of an affluent suburbia, the legislature stepped in and compelled the city to act as a utility, and at a low rate, thus ensuring the suburbs the advantages of city water without the disadvantage of sharing city burdens. The story exemplifies the general trend. Where state legislatures have been hostile (and they usually have been), the cities have been effectively blocked in their efforts to enlarge their borders so as to encompass the open land needed for growth and new construction. Most cities are isolated from the areas of new growth by an iron ring of incorporated municipalities and an iron wall of resistance to annexation.

Jay Forrester's *Urban Dynamics* outlines a scenario in which a city moves, if its territory is restricted, from empty land to a position where its land is used up. After this, if new construction takes place preponderantly outside its borders, it will increasingly come to possess the older and obsolescent residential, commercial, and industrial structures of the area. As these structures age the costs of maintaining them will increase, while the revenues they can command will decline. Wealthier residents will seek new and more fashionable housing beyond the city's borders, taking their tax-paying capacity with them. With the departure of the wealthy the city begins to be unfashionable. Middle-class elements follow the fashion leaders and so do the shops that cater to them, leading to losses in the city's retail trade. Obsolescence of residences is paralleled by obsolescence of industrial structures, and the multistory narrow bay lofts of an earlier day are deserted for single-story plants permitting layouts more suitable to the new technology. The relocation of industry reduces both the tax base and number and alters the kind of jobs available in the city. The change in the location of upper- and middle-class residence, of commerce and industry, alters the balance between professionals and businessmen, workers and the underemployed and unemployed.

These changes create, in Forrester's view, a systemic logic that leads to stagnation. More and more the politics of the city is dominated by the wants and needs of the underemployed and unemployed, but, however humane in motivation, such acts are ultimately counterproductive. For the economic key to the city's health is the balance between new and expanding, mature and declining industry. Public policies that manage the city's allocation of space and incentives in such a way as to discourage the location of new and expanding industry and to encourage the removal of such industry as it has lead to a further concentration of poverty, underemployment, and unemployment. Though in classical economics an underemployed or unemployed labor force should by itself in the long run generate a sufficient demand for its eventual employment, as Keynes said in the long run we are all dead. The long-run possibilities of stagnation have proved considerable, more than perhaps even the most ardent disciple of Milton Friedman would willingly endure. Forrester's model shows with powerful logic how a city with limited land would gradually become an island of poverty and obsolescence in a metropolitan sea of prosperity and new construction if it failed to manage its real estate in such a way as to forestall the fatal drift.

Former Mayor Collins of Boston, an early convert to urban renewal, who wrote an introduction to Forrester's book, must have found this elegant rationalization of urban renewal a reassuring vindication of his policies. Forrester strongly implies that the bias of a democratic political system is such that once the balance of the society is tipped toward the underemployed and the unemployed, public policies designed in their favor are almost bound to augment the forces of stagnation. This too must have struck a sympathetic note with Mayor Collins who experienced the ingratitude of Boston and Massachusetts voters.

Forrester's scenario might make one wonder how the cities of our democratic past avoided the political undertow leading to stagnation. Were the politicians of an earlier day more prescient of the economic danger or more capable of holding to a correct course despite democratic pressure and the allure of seemingly humanitarian but actually meretricious policies? Most likely not.

A more crass economic explanation of the older city's ability to avoid stagnation and maintain its economic and social balance is more persuasive. This explanation requires no assumption of superior fortitude, capacity, or wisdom on the part of the earlier political rulers, but depends for its logic on a profound and pervasive alteration in locational values, which (along with the cities' inability to expand to vacant land or annex territory) left the city the residuary legatee of downward mobility and obsolescence. As long as locational values in the city were high, land would be put to its highest economic use and lesser uses, if by chance they arose, would be priced out of the market. Where these values are still high, private enterprise, as on Park Avenue, razes valuable standing structures to replace them with still more valuable ones—and it does this without subsidy or urban renewal. The academic groves of Harvard and M.I.T. are unburdened of the residences of the poor by the housing demand of liberal students and faculty. (The effect of which demand the students and faculty themselves indignantly protest.) Indeed, by letting nature take its course, Cambridge would rapidly move, from a half-slum to a homogenized upper-class suburb. But Park Avenue and Cambridge are exceptional cases of a strong and enduring demand for the land of a central city and an older suburb. For the most part a demand exists only in highly special circumstances.

The older central city and the older suburb were stable to the extent they were when their land values were high because of their position in the transport technology of their day. While transport limited the availability of land the downward mobility of central-city property use would be checked through its replacement by new construction, as on Park Avenue today.

With the automobile and the truck came a transport revolution that opened up wide areas of cheap, vacant land for residential and industrial use. Hemmed in, for the most part, by a wall of incorporated suburbs, the central city and the older suburb were prevented from expanding to this open land. The resulting decline in their real estate values, and hence in their tax base, meant that, except in rare instances it was no longer profitable to replace standing structures of any value with new construction. So we began to witness property abandonment—land and structures with some seeming economic use left by their owners much as if they were curiales of the late Roman Empire seeking to escape their onerous burden to the state. The city and the older suburb became a concentrated mix of all the older downward mobile land uses of the metropolitan area attracting in growing and disproportionate numbers the population associated with these uses. Whereas the older city of the past contained within it the whole range of the country's nonagricultural population, the contemporary central city concentrates the extremes—the very wealthy who can insulate themselves from their surroundings with their wealth, and the poor and the discriminated against who have nowhere else to go. Moreover, whereas the older city contained within it a full range of jobs, the present city is increasingly cut off from the growing edge of the job market.

The fate of stagnation that Jay Forrester's analysis predicts hangs over large parts of older cities that are still economically vital, such as New York. The equilibrium analysis of such economists as Milton Friedman would see in the underemployment and unemployment of large elements of the labor force in older cities the pernicious result of well-meaning but fatuously meretricious public policy. If we did not pay so much relief, if we did not price marginal labor out of the market by unrealistically high minimum wages, and if we did not foolishly inhibit sweat-shop employers, Claude Brown would have to push the cart for Goldberg; economic sanctions would compel him and his ilk to shape up or else.

Followers of the Milton Friedman approach are frequently accused of hardness of heart toward the poor. They could with considerable justification point to the liberal policies of the nation's farm program as a monstrous analog. Just as grain is kept off the market and stored to jack up the price of grain sold, so people are stored off the labor market to keep up the price of union labor at the expense of those involuntarily unemployed by minimum wage and other restrictions. They could point out that these underemployed and unemployed are stored in public housing when available and in far worse quarters when, as most often, not. And they could say that these unfortunates are turned over to the tender mercies of cops and social workers to be kept in order and out of sight and off the conscience of a society that condemns them to a life of despised dependency marginal to or outside of the world of work. They could point out, as have Frances Piven and Richard Cloward,[2] that the slum landlord is a convenient and phony devil behind which to hide the unwillingness or inability of the society to provide housing of a quality it defines as standard for the poor. (Indeed when the city of New York took over slum property under similar economic compulsions it behaved much like the slum landlord its ideology condemned.)

Finally, the followers of Milton Friedman might maintain that the sweat-shop employer is a far better friend of the poor than the social worker and the humanitarian liberal. A relation of economic exploitation is ultimately far less degrading than one of dependency, even when the dependency is given a sociological sugarcoating. The worker, by virtue of having something of value to exchange with the sweat-shop employer and the society he represents, has some bargaining edge, however slight, with employer and society. Cutting him off from the world of work and transforming him into something less than a member of Marx's industrial reserve army, however much his paper legal rights, is to render him powerless indeed. The dependency, moreover, is destructive for the dependent and likely to be destructive for those who are given the task of acting as his keepers, however this may be disguised as service. The society ultimately will be niggardly, if not absolutely then surely by the standard of relative deprivation, the standard by which the dependent is bound to judge his condition.

Outside the labor market, the dependent loses skills and more important, his self-respect and capacity to work. Still more serious, the condition of dependency profoundly affects their families and their children, creating the conditions for Rainwater's and Oscar Lewis's culture of poverty.

But of course an indictment such as this cuts too deep and implies too much to be made seriously by those as close to establishment liberalism as the followers of Friedman.

In the past society did not set high standards for the living conditions of its poor. But neither did it goad its poor with the pronouncement of high standards which it had no serious intention of putting into effect. Our standards of poverty, as Anthony Downs has pointed out, are in reality based on two points of departure, which, if followed, lead to widely differing results: One standard starts from a minimally acceptable market basket of food and adds on from that. Even this produces a figure of around $3,000 for a family of four, a figure that a recent White House conference said should come to at least $5,000 for minimum adequate nutrition. At this confusion of need with the feasible the political sponsors of the conference threw up their hands. But as Downs shows, we have also been operating on a housing standard of poverty, and this shows an even more serious gap between the standards used to measure need and the dollar income that would be required to purchase or rent such housing. To purchase or rent standard new or rehabilitated housing the poor would need annual incomes in excess of $7,000.[3] It is readily to be seen why those concerned with welfare have avoided facing up to Downs's point. To do so would either quickly demonstrate the radical unfeasibility of the goal or the utopian nature of the housing standards.

As Downs's essay in "Agenda for the Nation" clearly shows, the Johnson administration's housing goals, the first

in which program was related to the stated measures of
need, were hopelessly unrealistic. To achieve the goals in
the amount and within the timetable of legislation would
have required the kind of national effort that was ex-
pended on winning World War II—which was not only
unlikely but in view of other important unmet needs,
highly undesirable. These facts were neither unknown to the
Department of Housing and Urban Development nor to
the sponsors of the legislation. The best defense of what
might be viewed as a cynical hoax on the poor is that in
the bureaucratic gamesmanship of Washington it is best to
stake out a high claim and then settle for what part of it
you can get appropriated. That after all is the way things
are done, and if it leads to cynicism, frustration, and rage
among the blacks, the young, and bubble-headed professors, so much the worse for them. They should grow up
and learn that, in the words of Wendell Willkie, "Campaign
oratory is just campaign oratory."

Cynicism among the blacks, the young, and the intellectuals is not a small price to pay for the way the game is
played in Washington, but there are other and equally unfortunate effects. An unreal and unattainable program may
not only block the achievement of attainable goals; it can
also hide the ill effects it produces under a fog of benevolent rhetoric. We all now know that, as Scott Greer maintains after study of the program,[4] the country has spent up-
wards of $3 billion to radically reduce the housing
available to the poor through its urban renewal program.
What we do not know is how much an unrealistically high
set of middle-class housing standards has done to retard
the construction of moderate-cost housing. Only belatedly
are we recognizing that the mobile homes are the only
product of the housing industry that comes anywhere near
what the bulk of the people can afford.

Detroit would have been well advised to go beyond ad-

vertising in its attempts to legislate middle-class taste and prices. It should have had enacted—perhaps there is still time—an automobile code. What if the public should learn of and come to like the Deux Chevaux? Bernard Frieden, in his perceptive study, *The Future of Housing in The Older Neighborhoods*,[5] shows how the American urban housing stock and housing condition were vastly improved in the post-World War II period. In his essay in *The Metropolitan Enigma* he points out that, with housing as with automobiles, the characteristic method of providing for all but the wealthier Americans is the secondhand market. Such housing, he points out, has not been bad.[6] In this he is probably right, though one may well wonder whether a poor man can afford to maintain adequately an aging middle-class house let alone a mansion. (Though no worse than the cost of maintaining an aging Cadillac, the individual's investment is vastly different and the social effects on the city, while not wholly dissimilar—aging Cadillacs can be eyesores and dangerous—are more serious.) But his major point, that providing housing through the used housing market has resulted in housing moving en masse from group to group in a process of ethnic and social succession, is critical.

Unlike used cars that move freely on the same highways with all the rest, new and old, expensive or cheap, used housing is tied to the land in the neighborhood in which it was built. The downward mobile older housing exists in large numbers and in particular places. This ensures that all those who because of income or discrimination find this the only housing available to them will live in these places willy-nilly, not because they want to but because they have to. When Forrester suggests that we should right the unbalanced concentration of the underemployed and unemployed poor and blacks in our built-up cities we are faced with the unstated and unanswered questions:

"Where else would we put them?" and "How could they (or for that matter, how could we) afford to provide the massive alternative accommodations their removal would require?"

If the housing segregation of the poor and blacks in our central cities were simply a problem of inadequate revenues to meet the high service costs of a low tax-paying, high service-requiring population transfer payments from other units of governments might be the solution. It might. But this will scarcely happen at the metropolitan level with governments as they are now constituted. Nor, given the balance of power in state legislatures, are these bodies likely to go in for what might well amount to a major redistribution of the state's income. Nor is it likely that the national government will open its coffers, already strained by war, defense and inflation. And even if by some unlikely chance we were able to pump money into the cities, we do not know whether the money would buy the results we wish. Carl Stokes, the Negro mayor of Cleveland, in a moment of candor made President Nixon gasp by stating that "Money will help us do the things we know how to do. But what do you do about the things you don't know how to do?" [7] When teenagers disrupt a high school, what do you do? Call in the National Guard? You can buy any honey with money—or can you? And these things we do not know how to do, for which there are no ready made solutions for money to buy, are the important things.

Mayor Stokes's wisdom, born of tragic conflict in his city, is rare among American mayors. More usual is the position of New Haven's famed Richard Lee, who, reviewing a recent book by Mayor Lindsay, underscored the all important matter of money. This is scarcely surprising since the seemingly all important task of the nation's mayors, as of other family heads, is finding the hard to come by cash to meet, if only in part, a burgeoning multitude of clamor-

ous demands. The nation's cities have become enormous businesses, purveying a range of services of the most varied and (increasingly) expensive kind. But unlike businesses, their wares are not for the most part paid for by their consumers nor are the services they produce of a kind, quality, and amount that would be dictated by normal market considerations. Oddly enough, a middle-class society has chosen to consume a rapidly expanding proportion of its income in the form of public goods.

Mayors are everywhere confronted by clamorous pressure groups and their bureaucratic allies pressing for funds to perform, maintain, and expand services that by received opinion and commonly held standards are desirable. With an insufficient bank account the mayor must somehow judge among these eager claimants and budget with his conscience and his electoral fortunes as a guide.

All this raises fascinating questions as to how in practice one operationalizes some concept of a public interest. Meyerson and Banfield, in their *Politics, Planning and the Public Interest*,[8] speculate that the rational self-interest of Chicago's Democratic machine might have had as likely an approximation to an operationally meaningful concept of the public interest as any realistically available alternative. Like the theories of the classical economists this sees the public interest as in the long run having to be brought about, if at all, through the unintentional effects of the pursuit of their self-interest by the key actors involved. There is reason to doubt that contemporary mayors, positioned as they are as conspicuous but weakly powered birds of civic passage, have either the self-interest or the capacity to further it by furthering a defensible conception of a long-term public interest.

The city, in complex relation with other local governments and state and nation, has in an ever-expanding sector of our society come to replace the economic market.

And in this replacement mayors, and to a lesser degree city councils, have unwillingly taken on the role of the market to ensure the production and allocation of public goods. But whereas in the case of the free competitive market of the classical economist there was at least a theory that sought to explain how the unintended result of the rational self-interest of the actors would be publicly beneficial, no such theory exists to explain the beneficent logic of the city. Indeed in a recent piece in *The Public Interest*,[9] James Wilson shrewdly remarks that mayors tend to perform for their audience rather than their constituency, for the Ford Foundation, the federal bureaucrats, the suburban, Park Avenue, and campus do-gooders and campus intellectuals rather than the mass of the inhabitants of their cities. They do this because, given their limited tenure on power and their future career potential, a politics of conspicuous gestures and projects has more to offer than a serious attempt to organize a constituency power base from which to attack fundamental problems.

The inadequacy of mayor and council not only leads to a clamorous demand for funds from outside sources—neither mayor nor council has the political strength to raise major sums from local sources except as forced to do so—but more importantly leads to a constant inflation of costs accompanied by a decline in at least the publicly perceived quality of services. Municipal transportation is a good example. It is the wonder of economists that a vital economic necessity such as transportation in an affluent society cannot pay its way at the fare box. Every logical model they make shows that it can. But the political transformation of the market, first with the public regulation of private transport, then with public takeover, radically transforms the nature of the operation. Thus we have the Long Island Railroad, traversing a corridor of ideally high density in an economically affluent society, in a condition

in which no one is satisfied—not riders, employees, or politicians. This curious result may be called the Czechoslovak effect of stagnant bureaucracy. It can be duplicated in the more serious matter of the schools, where with a constant demand for funds there is a sickening sense of regression and declining productivity. Neither pupils, teachers, nor parents are happy with the result.

Weakly powered and motivated mayors are poorly equipped to replace the market and preside effectively over an expanding municipal socialism, a socialism that, like many abroad, is unblessed by its putative beneficiaries. In practice, as Sayre and Kaufman's study of New York shows,[10] the typical thrust is toward the self-contained and self-directed professional bureaucracy running its own empire. In the name of good government, civil service, and professionalism and with the aid of the civic minded and the media, bureaucrats have successfully demanded uncontrolled self-direction. Mayors and politicians have been asked to keep their noses out of affairs they were professionally unequipped to understand and get on with the business of finding the money. This could work as long as the cities were burgeoningly affluent and the public sector was small, but today neither of these conditions any longer applies. Now the cost and productivity of the public sector are painful questions.

The rewards of the political system—and the incentives of its top executives—differ from those of business; how much only a close student of the modern corporation could say. But what does seem clear is that, in government, issues of cost control are rarely raised and issues of productivity still more rarely. In part this represents a politically expedient abdication before the powerful claims of professionalism. Education is surely a good example, though it exists in many other places. Thus people in the business have long known that money spent on fire prevention would do far more good than money spent on equipment, but fire departments resist such a change and the political gain from mobilizing the public support necessary to make the change never seems worth the effort. The fact is the motivations of politics accord but poorly with those necessary to resist an inherent tendency to inflate costs and reduce efficiency.

In addition to problems of costs and productivity the municipal decision-making process must also somehow determine what public goods will be produced and how these goods are to be allocated among its diversified citizenry. Clearly, a principal problem of the central city is its inability to provide within its boundaries the range and quality of public goods, for example, policing and schools, that many civic consumers of metropolis demand. Hence, the fragmentation of the metropolitan area, however dysfunctional in other respects, meets the demand for a varied range of public goods. With widely disparate incomes it is not surprising that formally equal citizens have widely differing tastes in public goods and widely differing effectiveness in their political as in their economic demands.

The fragmented governments of the metropolitan area and the central city command too few resources to manage effectively a municipal socialism that is neither recognized as such in our ideology nor planned for in the structure and capacity of our governments. Added bit by bit, the services of our society amount to a species of welfare state, a term that only yesterday, if then or now, lost the odium it had for Senator Taft and President Eisenhower. Since the municipal welfare state has come on us without much thought, we have shown little concern over what was to replace the market as allocator and enforcer of economizing on the part of political leaders and their bureaucratic enterprises. In this we have met a fate similar to that of the East European Communists, whence the term "Czechoslovak effect." This term expresses the stagnant, costly, unenterprising, consumer-be-damned behavior of centralized, irresponsible, and unresponsive bureaucracies. Recognition of the problem has finally dawned behind the Iron Curtain despite Communist dogma and is exemplified in the writings of Lieberman in the Soviet Union. But pursuing these ideas so threatened the Soviet powers that the Czechoslovakian move to put a humane face on socialism was crushed.

Recognition of bureaucratic drag has grown in this country. The President's Committee on Juvenile Delinquency and the Ford Foundation sponsored an array of change agents designed to force innovation on the entrenched bureaucracies of the public schools and welfare. In doing so they helped give rise to the ideology of maximum feasible participation. Christopher Jencks has even proposed that we provide the consumers of educational public goods with dollar ballots to stimulate salutory competition in a monopolistic educational market.[11] Hopefully, private-enterprise educational T.V.A.'s might, through the yardstick of competition, show that measurable educational productivity could be achieved at reasonable costs.

Given the ineffectiveness of present political controls to make public bureaucratic enterprise respond with service of quality and at reasonable cost, it is scarcely surprising that the market power of the citizen's dollar should seem a more promising means of increasing his leverage than his vote. On both sides of the Iron Curtain there is a common problem of putting a humane face on socialism. Michael Harrington has said that in America we have socialism for the rich and private enterprise for the poor.[12]

Our local political system, as much of the rest, was designed to play nightwatchman to laissez-faire capitalism. It has grown by inadvertence and without any careful reconsideration of its premises, either ideological or structural, into a massive public goods-producing enterprise. Power in this system largely results in the bureaucratic enterprises and their allies who have staked an effective claim to some market, education, police, welfare, or whatever.

As governmental activities these enterprises are regarded as service industries, and as service industries they are not expected to function with increasing productivity. If you want more—in quality or quantity—of their wares you pay more. If wages generally go up in the private sector, policemen and teachers expect theirs to go up likewise, and they do not expect their increases to come out of an increase in productivity. Further, in the public sector, for the most part pricing is not used to relate supply to economic demand. Mass transport is frequently subject to bulk-line pricing, designed to provide a merit good to the poor, thus providing all those who could afford to bear the economic cost with a large and unneeded subsidy.

With little politically effective incentive to increase the productivity and profitability of its operations, the city is caught between its inability to control its costs and ration its wares by rational pricing, on the one hand, and an inelastic tax structure, on the other. As long as prices and wages go up in the private sector, city costs and the wages of city employees are under heavy pressure. Private sector wages can be partly offset by increases in labor productivity and what cannot can be passed on along with material prices through price increases. But the management of cities rarely wins a battle over increasing the efficiency of public employees, and user charges, even on such clearcut items as water and parking, are rarely invoked. Faced with rising taxes of a highly regressive and income inelastic sort, citizens increasingly resist paying the piper for bureaucratic enterprise whose performance seems both costly and shoddy. Public employees who see their incomes steadily falling behind teamsters and the building trades regard their jobs as poor and their prospects as worse. Politicians find both employee demands and citizen reluctance to be taxed further an impasse whose only ready escape is a handout from some more affluent or less tax-sensitive jurisdiction.

In a society that regards itself as affluent, it seems hard to believe that there are worthy and legitimate human needs for which there are not enough resources. Downs's point about the Johnson housing program is in order here. There is a radical disjunction between our process for formulating human needs and criticizing our shortcomings in attaining them and the equally important task of assessing priorities among competing needs and budgeting them in relation to our available resources. We have thrust the job of the market on a politics that is ill prepared, if prepared at all, to accept the burden. And we have done so in a climate of widespread belief that scarcity and cognitive competence had ceased to be problems. Such an atmosphere lends itself to the cynicism of the Johnson housing program or to the projects without program of urban renewal. We are never honest with ourselves as to what we can afford and what, given what we can afford, our values tell us we should afford. More than anything, we suffer from this lack of honesty with ourselves and one another.

The divorce of politics from economics has tended to leave us without any appreciation of the budget as an ethical document. Yet a budget that is a plan, and a plan that is a meaningful embodiment of social purposes related to both needs and capabilities, is the beginning of both civic education and civic honesty. A critical deficiency of the metropolitan anticity, as Professor Haar and his associates pointed out, is its inability to plan, to entertain consciously held purposes. In this it resembles in its actions the forces of nature and is poles apart from a citizen community capable of deliberate moral choice.

The nation-state of modern capitalism has opened the

walls of the older city to the almost full force of the regional and national market. In the process, the cities and states have become open economies. John Dyckman and Catherine Wurster have both argued [13] that in spite of this openness the states are not without means to affect the course of their economies. The fairly massive state investments in roads, hospitals, utilities, education, and other public works remain unharnessed to any clearly articulated set of goals and plans for their attainment. As both Professor Dyckman and Mrs. Wurster have noted, the capital expenditures of the states are large in absolute if not relative amounts. Though they do not approach the federal magnitudes, they are far from inconsequential. Yet, for the most part, these investments remain unused as tools for improving the effectiveness of the state's economy. Despite much planning, states have no serious economic plans. Their helplessness as mere reflexes of the national economy is accepted almost without question—perhaps even with a sigh of relief as absolving state leadership from any serious responsibility for the functioning of the economies of the states.

What is true of the states is even more true of the cities. The older city, even when only a quasiindependent polity, was an economic enterprise with a shrewd concern for its sources of livelihood. Markets, trade routes, food and water supply were all concerns of the city as a political business watching over the livelihood of its inhabitants. The drastic alteration of the city in the nation-state, its opening wide to the market, left it the role of municipal purveyor of public goods, a housekeeping enterprise. This latter function was of minor import during the nineteenth century, though cholera and plagues made water supply important if cities were to be more than human bonfires fed with bodies from the countryside. Raymond Vernon and his associates,[14] studying New York, found that apart from the Erie Canal, a state undertaking, perhaps the Brooklyn Bridge was the only public work to have real economic impact.

The Vernon studies yield the distinct impression that the city and its polity exist as an epiphenomenon to an economy that it did little to bring into being and can do little to affect for good or ill. Perhaps today, observing the threats of massive disinvestment from the city, Vernon and his associates would see skyrocketing municipal costs, employee strikes and walkouts, and the fear of crime as factors that seriously affect location. Here, perhaps, is an instance of the classical economic view that the state can do harm by its meddling, that even with the best of intentions it is likely to do no good. What is interesting in the Vernon studies and others dealing with location is their dim view of the potential of a positive urban economic policy. This view, accepted by city officials and leaders, has tended to permit, and even encourage, them to avoid consideration of the functioning of the urban economy as beyond their power or perhaps as not existing as an economy in any significant sense.

The growth of the metropolitan area has also seemed to deprive the city of any appreciable power over its economic fate. The metropolitan area is a housing market and a labor market. The city internalizes neither the places where many of the people who work within it live nor the places where many of the people who live within it work, or might work. Insofar as there is a true local economy, it is that of the metropolitan area. This is an economy that now exerts more control over the city than the city is able to exert over it. Though the working of the economy within the city is to a degree under the control of the city's government, the working of the metropolitan economy is under no over-all control short of the state or nation. Though the states have with national assistance and prodding set up regional planning areas, they have neither themselves formulated effective economic plans nor seen to the formation of such plans by the regions they have set up, let alone having the plans seriously implemented. The metropolitan area then remains largely an economy whose functioning, while controlled by the national economy, is in significant part determined by the peculiar structure of the metropolitan market with all the rigidities its political structure entails. A major value of the market celebrated by the classical economists was its efficiency in the utilization and allocation of resources. The unemployment and underemployment of important elements of the potential labor force and the seemingly wasteful premature obsolescence of housing, business structures, and the capital stored up in organizations, schools, governments, churches, and the like make the operation of many metropolitan markets suspect.

Thus Sol Linowitz points to the growth of low and unskilled jobs preponderantly in the suburbs where the city's and many of the older suburb's residents can neither secure housing nor afford to commute.[15] S. M. Miller and Pamela Roby cite Dorothy Newman's study, *The Decentralization of Jobs,* to the effect that "currently it would cost a worker in Harlem $40 a month to commute by public transportation to work in an aircraft plant in Farmingdale, L. I., in a parts plant in Yonkers, Westchester, or in a basic chemical plant on Staten Island." [16] Presumably, a well-functioning market would bring men as well as materials together, in both cases meeting the costs of transport. Possibly the present market would do that in the long run; certainly that is what the devotees of the market as a cure-all would claim, barring ill-advised government action. Unfortunately, what government action should be desisted from remains unspecified, and if that action taken in the past has irretrievably spoiled the self-regulating mechanism, other remedies must be sought. In the long run, we are, as Keynes said, all dead, and meaningful experiments must be feasible in shorter time spans.

What we do not know are the actual outcomes of the metropolitan market as they affect the lives of specifiable people and groups of people along such key dimensions as health, housing, jobs, income, and education. Without such an inventory of performance it is impossible to evaluate with any degree of accuracy the outcomes of the metropolitan public choice market and its governments. Appreciation of the existing incentive system and cognitive maps of the institutional actors in the metropolitan system could give us some understanding of how it acts as a complex role-producing and role-allocating mechanism. And with such an understanding of the characteristics of the market we might choose to retain it with alterations, but to rig its action in the service of a set of goals selected by a consciously and carefully chosen agency for making our choice.

John Dyckman, speaking of his own work and that of Richard Burton of the Urban Institute, says,

Our work on regional econometric models long ago convinced us that virtually nothing is known about the way that local economies contribute to the national economy—all the emphasis is unfortunately on local "shares." At some point, obviously, the federal government has to get something to share, and it must expand the pie by expanding local economies. The latter mechanism is increasingly obscured by all our economic accounting.[17]

A picture of the local economy, derived from a breakdown of national shares, is a statistical aggregate that gives no clue as to the patterned system of localized interaction. Having a statistic rather than an explanatory theory of the local phenomena, we have no conception of what logic is at work and how that logic might be altered to entail more desired outcomes. It may be that much of our inability to plan at the local level results from an economic technology of national accounts that yields no relevant information for local action.

The assault on poverty directed by the Council of Economic Advisers, for example, was confined to the crude, hopelessly inflationary, and in the end inadequate tools of macro-Keynesianism. An attempted investment exercise during the early Kennedy years was viewed with alarm by business, according to Andrew Shonfeld, and hastily backed off from. A manpower exercise, similar to ones familiar from the war years, sponsored by the Department of Labor, was more favorably received. In the event, however, it failed to displace the macro- and fiscal fixation of the Council of Economic Advisers and the other planning authorities in Washington. Swedish manpower planning has yet to catch on seriously in Washington though the administration's manpower bill of 1969 might have been a move in that direction. Given the importance attached to it as compared with revenue-sharing there is little question of the present priorities. One might hope that the priorities reflect a judgment as to comparative political expediency rather than comparative social and economic importance.

Though the metropolitan area is usually looked at as an embryonic government that ought to be brought into being because of its potential for largely internalizing the physical or seemingly physical problems of water distribution, sewerage, the utilities, and transport, an even more important reason, though one not often given, is the fact that it is the most important local labor market. The labor market for good or ill is the most potent allocator of roles in society. As Chalmers Johnson remarks in his essay on revolutions,[18] it is the legitimacy of the system of role allocation that underpins the social order. Since the labor market through its allocation of jobs determines in a major way the allocation of income, it also determines the access of individuals and their families to housing, education, and health. Because, as previously noted, housing to a great degree determines access to education and education to the job and the job to income, the working and interaction of housing and education are largely determinative of role assignment in the society.

In our society the workings of education and the labor market have both been treated as sacred cows to be worshipped rather than put to purposive use by the society they are supposed to serve. Assessment of the function of both the metropolitan labor market and its system of education can bring to light how well these institutions are serving to mobilize, develop, and utilize the potential of the area's labor force. A manpower plan that sought the fullest utilization of the potential of the human resources of a metropolitan area would make sense both in furthering the prosperity of the total population of the area and effectively attacking some of the principal social problems at their source. Such a plan also has the virtue of providing a rational means for coordinating other forms of planning, such as housing, transportation, and the other utilities to the most important metropolitan goal—the fullest and best employment of its people. As a start, this seems the best place to begin. In their perceptive book, *The Future of Inequality*, Miller and Roby rightly point to status, self-respect, and the respect of others as important aspects of the problem of inequality.[19] But for most the job and its outcomes are the critical immediate issue. A good society will ultimately be concerned with creating the possibility of its people utilizing their talents in a developing role structure that gives them the fullest scope. Here the Greek view of the city as a means to the self-realization of its citizens is still relevant.

There is a tendency to despair of the possibility of creating metropolitan governments. Quite obviously they would threaten the present use of the metropolitan area as a means of validating the segregated consumption of public goods by citizens with differing incomes. The metropolitan area is a battleground for the conception of equal citizens getting equal public services vs. the conception of people with unequal incomes desiring to spend those unequal incomes on a quantity and quality of public goods they do not wish to share with others of lesser income. Yet what is acceptable in the private market, "He who has, gets," is at least formally obnoxious to the equal protection of the laws among citizens, even citizen consumers. The California Supreme Court has given this recognition by finding that state delegation of the function of education to local governments, depending on property taxation in areas of gross fiscal disparity, results in such large differences in educational expenditures as to violate the constitutional provision for the equal protection of the laws. If this decision is upheld by the U.S. Supreme Court, as seems likely to occur, the existing gross inequalities among the local governments' fiscal capacities to perform the state functions entrusted to them will be open to attack. Whether the court will be able to restrict its concern to education seems doubtful. What is involved here is the same logic as that behind the Goldenberg report on Toronto Metro. The equality norm among citizens conflicts with segregation of public goods consumption achieved through the fragmentation of local government and the property tax.

If the problem were merely the consumption of amenities such as swimming pools, segregated public goods consumption would be a mere irritation in a democratic society. But, as noted earlier, the segregation of public goods relates to education, which, however much it may seem to a mere consumer good, is in our credentialist society the necessary passport to college and job. Without some realistic semblance of equality of opportunity the uneasy relation between the achievement norm of the society justifying inequalities of income and the equality norm of free citizens is upset and the legitimacy of the social order based on it comes into question.

The ideal thrust toward equalizing the condition of citizens within the same government with respect to their enjoyment of public services is powerful. Its logic operates in the deferential democracy of Canada, and it is at work in the rhetoric, legislation, and court decisions of the United States. But it would be better for all of us if, along with the kind of thrust represented by the Goldenberg report on Toronto Metro pressing for equal service standards, we had a thrust toward the metropolitan government as a means of achieving a more efficient and humanly desirable local economy than the present metropolitan public goods market is likely to create. The emphasis on the metropolitan area merely as a redistributive agent for the purchase of standard services for all runs the danger that the government of the area will, like that of New York City, show scant concern with the economy and efficiency of its resource utilization. It is likely that the states and the nation will increasingly come to recognize the importance of metropolitan areas as critical population centers for both levels of government. They need to be recognized as local economies, and the governments that will come to structure them had best be concerned with the impact of their investment in public goods on the local economy's performance.

A full employment program that makes the fullest and best use of the metropolitan area's population, particularly its youth, makes as much sense as the land-use planning that is most commonly cited as a major appropriate objective for metropolitan planning. In fact, manpower planning is a necessary condition for the intelligent formulation of other plans. When and if the federal government adopts a measure such as the Nixon administration's manpower bill of 1969, it is entirely likely that the states will use it not only in a state-wide plan but in plans regionalized to the states' labor markets, in many cases their metropolitan areas. With a reasonable inventory of metropolitan areas' human resources and their existing degree of utilization and underutilization, it should become possible to formulate reasonable targets for the more effective utilization of the existing stock of manpower, the upgrading of its capabilities, and the development of a more satisfactory job mix and array of occupations. Once the society has both the knowledge of how, and how well, it is employing its people, it will want to know whether and how it could do better.

For the metropolitan area and the city are complex opportunity structures in which social slotting mechanisms and incentive systems make probable the employment of people in a wide variety of occupations, including many that are regarded as undesirable, such as crime, drug addiction, and dependency. Moralistic explanations of these socially undesirable behaviors, such as those given in Banfield's *Unheavenly City*,[20] have a measure of truth and usefully point to the individual's adoption of an ethic of immediate gratification as an important explanation for his fate. But they implicitly avoid the question of society's responsibility. In this Banfield joins forces with Booker Washington and Malcolm X, who from different perspectives chose to emphasize the individual's capacity, whatever the conditions, to significantly affect his fate. Scott Greer suggests that for men,

When they fail, and fail again, they have little recourse to a tool kit of concepts and techniques. Under such circumstances they adopt, or reaccept, a fatalism which is the age old recipe of humanity for surviving adversity. Thus the alternate (but not em-

pirically conflicting explanation) might be that the culture of
poverty is not a culture; it is the aggregated effects of failure to
be socialized into the game in such a way that you might win
on a small scale. Thus one becomes deculturated and fatalistic
—for good, pragmatic reasons from some points of view.[21]

What Greer is suggesting here is that such fatalism is
an understandable reaction on the part of those who adapt
in this way to the bleakness of their situation and the prospects that confront them. As Mollie Orshansky has remarked, when a man works all day, every day, every week
in the year, as many do, and still finds his family in poverty, it is scarcely surprising that he should become
discouraged. With the erosion of otherworldly religions
and of ethnic-integrated neighborhoods, there are few sup-
ports left that make the weary round bearable. Particularly
for a youth brought up in the advertising culture of an affluent consumerism such fardles bearing, in Hamlet's
phrase, seems a mug's game.

The urgent question, however, is whether their fatalism
must also be fatalistically accepted by society. Clearly, society suffers from the behavior the existing situation and
its perception engenders. In *Talley's Corner,* Elliot
Liebow [22] has given a graphic description of marginal men
who entertain the society's norm of a stable family but recognize the odds against achieving it, trying and failing and
trying again and failing, and adapting to the perceived
inevitability of failure. Rainwater's work also suggests that
for some the society's alternatives are so punishing in
terms of the likelihood of failure that to protect the self
a life style that softens the blows of expected defeat while
ensuring its occurrence is adopted. But even without the
apparatus of a sociological, psychological, or moralistic
perspective, a simple economic analysis of the occupations
open to classes and groups of people would predict the
adoption of the socially dysfunctional behavior that society

finds so costly. Where a quarter of the jobs available pay incomes below the poverty line, as in New York, Saint Louis, and other cities, and where in addition they are dirty, casual, and deadend in the bargain, it is understandable that, without the older religious motivation and with declining social pressure, only the lash of hunger will man them. Nathan Glazer has suggested [23] that New York, with a relatively easy and humane welfare program, is previewing the guaranteed income. It indicates, as he sees it, a massive moral change. Given the choice between welfare or poverty wages, many will take welfare.

Various elements of society, including the affluent middle class, the intellectuals, the politicians, and the media, have preached a doctrine that rejects the religious counsel of submission to providence and challenges the manliness of accepting with resignation a life of pointless marginal drudgery. Through its varying statistical marketbaskets of subsistance and minimal standards of decency for family living, society has implicitly and explicitly criticized the performance of an economy that makes even livelihoods officially regarded as minimal beyond the reach of many. When to the sections of the elite denouncing the conditions available to the poor is added the society's own ambivalence—on the one hand legislating welfare standards and on the other reneging on following them—moral confusion and anger are inevitable. Cloward and Piven have counseled, as perhaps the only way of forcing society to face up to the problem, the swamping of relief rolls by getting all legally entitled on them.

Those who make *The Unheavenly City* unheavenly are not only Banfield's deviants following an ethic of immediate gratification but all those who intentionally and unintentionally, as Alinsky recommends, "rub raw the sores of discontent." Seen from a larger perspective it is perhaps inevitable that the affluent should find the condition of the poor insufferable and teach the poor to find it insufferable too. The ugly spectacle of poverty is the more distasteful for our middle-class society since our economists and political leaders have long ago taught us we could afford to do without it. Yet a very high proportion of the jobs in the large city *are* dirty, deadend, casual, and pay below the poverty line. Some think we cannot do without these jobs and need an underclass to fill them, an underclass the culture of poverty provides. Gotbaum struck New York for a set of municipal employees, a third or more black and Puerto Rican, who cleaned the city's sewers, scrubbed the cages of the zoo, and emptied the bedpans of the hospitals. Their median income was $7,500. Such an income officially spells far less than a standard of modest comfort for a family of four. For housing in New York it is a disaster. And Gotbaum's union members are not by any means at the bottom of the ladder of American cities.

In many an American city black youths will graduate from or drop out of school—and it matters not much which—to struggle against unemployment rates ranging up to 40 per cent and more. Though some of this unemployment results from the administration's response to the inflation caused by the Vietnam War and its financing, in ordinary times things are not a great deal better. What response does one make to 40 per cent unemployment? When only a fraction of this happened to whites during the Great Depression the country was convulsed. Blacks unprepared to starve and unable or unwilling to take welfare (or dissatisfied with what welfare has to offer) may and will seek gainful illegal occupations. Whites will as well. Policies producing 40 per cent unemployment rate among youth are no more than an invitation to survive any way you can. By its actions and its failure to act society produces the crime, the drug addiction, the dependency, and the hustle from which its cities suffer.

Inevitably a job outlook as bleak as that confronting central-city youth also infects the whole educational system with a sense of frustration and futility. Despite all the rhetoric about education and jobs, the children learn from elder brothers and sisters and those on the street that the educational staircase leads nowhere. A city with inadequate legitimate occupational opportunities will find itself paying a heavy price for condemning many of its people to illegitimate occupations. Society is a teaching machine armed with carrot and stick. With illegal carrots the only fodder around, it has little else than a club—the police—with which to maintain its order.

The way the market presently operates would seem much in need of revision. A few thousand young blacks and whites find attractive occupations that do grave damage to the city. If the process that produces this in the central city is neither self-correcting nor altered by conscious policy there is no reason to believe that it will remain within the boundaries of the central city or the older suburb. It is little short of amazing that enormous investments in the city's stock of housing and business properties should be allowed to rapidly obsolesce, that billions should be spent on schools, youth programs, and police to little effect. A poorer society would be unlikely to afford such a luxury. The large corporations will leave places like New York less because they want to than because they feel they have to. The general loss in property values through premature blight is out of all proportion to the economic cost of alternative employment of those whose behaviors presently occasion the city's decay. The economy of the city is organized to permit and give incentive to the abandonment of millions of dollars in business and housing, to the fruitless expenditure of other millions in education and police and housing programs; yet the same economy that can spend these millions to no effective purpose cannot mount attrac-

tive alternative occupations to crime, idleness, dependency, and drug addiction. Perhaps without the lash of
hunger and scarcity and really savage repression we are
at a loss to alter the systematic outcomes of a process we
have neither the wit to understand nor the will to change.

The city has been subjected to a noble experiment far
more devastating than the earlier one of the Volstead era.
The older prohibition produced Capone and the gangsters;
some of the poor went blind or died drinking wood alco-
hol, and thousands were introduced into the arts of producing bathtub gin and home brew; but never in the dark-
est days of prohibition did we mass produce crime on the
streets by compelling those with a drinking habit to mug
someone to get the price of a drink. City jails are full of
prisoners who have committed robberies and assaults to
get the price of a fix.

Much of the crime problem appears to be a self-inflicted
wound the society needlessly and mindlessly inflicts on itself. Paul Lerman provides interesting evidence [24] that in
the treatment of the young for juvenile status offenses we
early on begin the process of producing criminals. Much of
our police effort is uselessly related to nuisances. Norval
Morris, Director of the Center for Studies of Criminal Justice of the University of Chicago, asserts that "the 2,000,000
arrests yearly in the country for public drunkenness—
which represent a third of all arrests—had little impact on
the problem and should be irrelevant to police." [25] Much
police effort is wasted on the enforcement of nuisance
laws. The major problem, as Morris points out, and the
one from which the cities suffer most seriously, is "the increase in violent crimes committed by youths between the
ages of 15 and 24 in inner city areas." However, current police methods based on a theory of deterrence are unlikely
to succeed. Morris has pointed to the shocking fact that "of
every 100 crimes committed in the United States only

about 50 were reported to the authorities. Those 50 crimes lead to an average of 12 arrests, 6 convictions and 2 persons sent to jail." [26] The efficiency of the present law enforcement system, even on its own terms, is woefully low.

Unfortunately, as in so many other social situations, the interests of the police and the prejudices of the public lead not to a reexamination of the problem and the efficacy of present policies but to hysterical calls for more of the same. As Morris remarks, "Marches against marijuana, wars on smut and strike forces against organized crime may look good to politicians, but they have nothing to do with the really serious problems of organized crime." [27] An economic interpretation of crime would treat it as a business and without undue impiety would recall that many of the nation's patriots were, under the laws of their day, criminals, smugglers, tax evaders, and worse. Taking the profit out of crime is a major way of stopping it, though in doing so many presently happily employed elements of the criminal justice system—detectives, courts, lawyers, press, legislators, and organizations—might, as Skolnik suggests in his *Justice Without Trial*,[28] lose individually satisfying if socially counterproductive activities.

Another approach to the problem of crime is to give alternative employment to people who are on the way to becoming or have become criminals. Ramsay Clark laments [29] that though we know that 80 per cent of the inmates of our prisons will become recidivists, we do next to nothing to make it possible for them to have the skills and opportunity to find a satisfactory legitimate occupation. An employment strategy would treat crime and drug addiction as occupations, occupations that would not be chosen by persons with more attractive alternatives. The police could be really useful here through their intimate knowledge of the population at hazard. If the police had constructive alternatives to either attempting to frighten or jail the population, it would be worth a great deal of society's resources to give them a more promising alternative system in which to refer and place the at-hazard population. The earlier youth are locked into a satisfying career ladder, the less likelihood of future trouble.

The older city is frequently treated by its political leaders as if it had no power over its fate and no choice but to wheedle and beg support for its growing deficits from state and federal governments. It is true that the city no longer contains the local labor market or even the greatest part of it within its boundaries; this limits, though it does not destroy, its leverage on that market and the public and private forces affecting it. But the city does have important resources within its power if only it had the leadership, knowledge, and political capacity to use them to constructive effect. Today, especially with the vogue of revenue-sharing, there is much talk about the fiscal mismatch between the city's needs and its fiscal resources, but the real mismatch may be between the way the city needs to use its resources and the way it actually uses them. As Lyle Fitch pertinently remarks,

When city budgets attempt to rise, as New York City's has, from $3.4 billion in 1964–65 to $9.1 billion in 1971–72 there is bound to be great strain even if New York is the nation's richest city and imposes every form of tax yet devised by the municipal imagination. And when the increase of expenditures is associated with 45% to 80+% increases in the average wages of major employee groups, a 113% increase in pension requirements, and a lively suspicion of sinking productivity in many sectors, the fiscal mismatch takes on new perspectives. Mismatch is hardly a suitable term for the relationship between a food supply which, even though substantial, is ultimately limited and a dinosaurian appetite which devours everything in sight and roars for more.[30]

New York is only an extreme case of the cost inflation of municipal government. It is paralleled elsewhere. Education, a principal component of the city's budget, reflects the trend.

> From Boston to Seattle, big city school officials are nearly unanimous in forecasting disaster unless additional sources of revenue are found. . . . The school budget in most cities has doubled or even tripled in the last 10 years. . . . The increasing cost of public education is attributable partly to inflation, partly to an increased demand for services. But mostly it can be laid to the rapidly rising salaries of teachers.[31]

The teachers are joined by police and firemen and now at long last by the very bottom of the public service proletariat. All these feel justified in seeking wages comparable to those prevailing in the private sector. Mayors and city fathers have to run hard merely to stay in the same place and irate tax payers find themselves asked to pay higher taxes frequently for fewer and poorer services.

This phenomenon, one of the root causes of the city's plight, has been explained by William Baumol in a classic article, "Macroeconomics of Unbalanced Growth; The Anatomy of Urban Crisis." [32] Baumol's thesis is essentially that the city is in the service industry and this industry is not characterized by increases in productivity. Frequently you have more teachers teaching fewer pupils to less effect at higher salaries. At best the ratio is likely to remain the same with wages going up. Wages are set in the public sector by reference to those paid in comparable jobs in the private sector. Teachers expect to be paid as much as truckdrivers and when truckdrivers get higher pay teachers want higher pay too. The hitch is that when truckdrivers get higher pay industry may offset the increase by increasing truckdrivers' productivity, somehow getting them to haul more ton-miles a week. And of course industry can pass on its increased labor costs in increased prices. But the city is stuck with the costs.

Though there is a certain amount of truth in Baumol's

thesis, there is also a good deal of doubt that cities are extracting—or, indeed they are even trying to extract—all possible use out of the existing technology. Lyle Fitch, former city administrator of New York City, states, "A recent study indicates that the cost of picking up refuse by New York City's highly mechanized sanitation department is three times the price quoted by private cartmen," and further that "down time on new city sanitation trucks is about 33% ; the same as for the trucks they replaced; apparently garages cannot handle the minimal maintenance necessary to keep new equipment in operating condition." [33] This is New York City, far from the worst run municipal enterprise in the country. More important than Baumol's thesis may be what Lyle Fitch and Henry Cohen see as a built-in lack of effective incentives to achieve efficient performance in the public sector.

Not only is the reward structure for individual employees such that they have little incentive to perform, but the over-all political system works to avoid effective cost control. Thus as Fitch acidly comments,

The Boston Metropolitan Transit Authority shows operating costs per passenger mile nearly twice those of other major transit systems, largely because of archaic labor practices, staffing patterns and work rules. Rather than seeking to improve matters by fairly obvious efficiency measures, the system has prevailed upon its congressional delegation to put pressures on the federal government for transit operating subsidies, which could soak up any conceivable amount of federal grant funds.[34]

This is obviously a public-choice mechanism powered by a set of political incentives that do not reward any misguided effort to economize. Civil service is largely in the control of powerful public employee unions and has become a job protection device. Many union-controlled services are vital, and a strike can paralyze the city. Moreover, the employee unions control a large block of votes in

New York City, according to Fitch some 20 per cent of the total votes cast in elections. The unions are not under the market controls and management incentives that exist in private industry.

In bargaining with the unions, officials make little attempt to relate wage increases to productivity. Legislators and most elected officials show far more interest in contracts, buildings, and jobs, the inputs of the political system, than in the outputs, the delivery of goods and services to the citizen. Such incentives do not lead to a rational concern with the well-being of most if not all the inhabitants of the city. The city is run like a colony and increasingly like an Indian reservation.

This process might seem suicidal in that the goose that lays the golden eggs is being cooked by those who depend on it for a livelihood. Yet a Freudian death urge is not unknown to union leaders and others whose individual and apparently rational and, more to the point, righteous demands produce a collective disaster. The slaughter of newspapers by typographical unions is well known. The long drawn out struggle of the railways with featherbedding and work rules is a struggle reminiscent both on the side of the unions and of management with that now occurring in the public sector. Public-choice theorists, economists, political scientists, and sociologists are prone to believe that there is a built-in homeostatic propensity in the system. But as they should have learned from an economist critic of the classical tradition, Keynes, equilibrium can occur at levels of stagnation. In such a situation unions—as in the railways—may prefer to hang on for dear life and squeeze the last nickel rather than join in a doubtful venture of restoring the enterprise to health at their expense. Businesses may find their profit in disinvesting and milking properties rather than in investing in the city and making their profit from activities that cause the city's economy to stabilize and grow. Increasing city costs can bring about tax rates, as in Newark and elsewhere, that make disinvestment seem the only rational response to a hopeless outlook. Under such circumstances well-nigh revolutionary political change may be necessary to avert the starvation in the banana plantation projected by Keynes.

The process is the harder to alter inasmuch as the actions of all the parties seem fair and reasonable. Employee unions see their members' living standard cut by inflation and outdistanced by gains in the private sector. In terms of the cost of living and what they see as the pay of comparable workers, their demands seem eminently fair and quite modest, and they are. This fact, however, does not mean that acceding to them without compensating productivity increases would not make the city or any other business go broke. The scoring system of union leaders and their union audience is how well they do for their members in competition with other unions for such gains as are to be made. They are concerned about wages, working conditions, and the maintenance and increase in the number of jobs and the size of the union membership on which their own prestige and power depend. They have little concern with how costs are to be met; that is someone else's business. The unions are also in many cases able to halt vital services on which the city's functioning depends. Teachers' strikes, garbage collectors' strikes, blue flu, and a growing number of other "labor actions" show just how vulnerable the large city has become to the blackmail of its employees. The public employees and their families are a substantial block of votes. For many purposes they are allied with the unions in the private sector and can count on their support in disputes with the city administration. Rarely, though there are instances, has organized labor felt responsible for ensuring the solvency of the enterprise by which it is employed. With the expansion of the public sector there is thus a built-in tendency for inflation and rising cost.

This tendency is one that existing political leaderships

have shown little ability to control. The rewards of politics, except in crisis, go all the other way. Brick and mortar, construction and jobs, are the stuff of politics. Effective quality output rarely pays off at the polls, and insistence on it can bring down the wrath of potent interests. The public, business, the press, and other levels of government may call for economy and efficiency, but none of these has the organized interest and staying power of those who concretely benefit from loose spending and waste. Besides, every one of the voices raised for economy and efficiency has its own pets and sacred cows that must be fed regardless of what, in the role of Portia, it proclaims. The incentives of the weakly based political birds of passage manning the top elective offices of the cities are primarily concerned with keeping the ship afloat, at least till they have got ashore. The operation is constantly one of shifts and contrivances, of bailing and buying time. The time that is bought never seems to be used or to suffice for a fundamental reform of the structure. The property tax on which the enterprise is largely based arouses pain in those who pay it. Others, the poor on whom it falls most heavily, frequently are unaware of how regressively the cities' major tax falls on them. If public-choice theory worked, the rising property tax would force reform on political leaders. Between pressure of the unions and pressure of the property tax the preferred out is postponement, borrowing, and increasingly the attempt to shift the fiscal burdens of the city to the state and federal governments.

One might ask why, faced with municipal bankruptcy, the city does not rethink the wisdom of its municipal expenditures. Any family faced with such a drastic imbalance between income and outgo would get the message and begin a process of selective retrenchment. But the city and its leaders do not behave like a family. The family, unless it breaks up, has to stick together. Not so the unwalled city. Faced with the choice of making a fight to change the city budget or disinvesting and leaving the city to its own resources, only a few businesses and citizens will choose to stay. An unwalled city produces insufficient loyalty among its residents to make it worth the cost in time, money, and risk to take the chance of throwing good money and good time after bad. Businesses, middle-class, and working-class follow one another out of the city—and the decaying suburb too. All are bewildered that spending money on good objectives should have such a sorry result.

The question arises whether much of what the city does amounts to more than well-intended, increasingly expensive patent medicines. Some services, such as education and police, may even be counterproductive. An education that at great expense turns out students who are not only illiterate but motivated to slovenly habits and rebellious attitudes is an expensive luxury for a city hard pressed to hold its productive sector. A police whose efforts serve to create a billion dollar illicit drug industry, fill the jails, and mass produce addicts who commit street crimes to secure the price of a fix is another expensive luxury for a city desperately concerned to hold businesses and middle- and stable working-class families among its inhabitants. A welfare program that serves as a scapegoat for the city's ills for business, middle class, blue-collar working class, and employee unions alike, and in addition serves to demoralize and degrade the poor is another expensive luxury for the hard pressed city.

The cost of these counterproductive patent medicines shows up in higher and higher taxes, but the benefits fail to show up in reduction in crime, a more effective labor force, or more efficient city services and other amenities. Under the circumstances it is not surprising that those who can, move. As Forrester's model predicts, the city homogenizes downward. Its productive sector and its productively employed decline. Those left are those who needs must stay, the mature and declining businesses, the trapped, the dependent and the increasingly custodial personnel, the keepers, teachers, cops, welfare workers, and the rest.

As Professor Burch of the Harvard Business School suggests,[35] the central city must find a new role. Since it can no longer contain within itself the full range of the older city, now spread throughout the metropolitan area, it must specialize. One specialty, although not suggested by Professor Burch, is as an Indian reservation or poor farm moved downtown, whose dependent population is supplemented by businesses that thrive by exploitating it —such illegitimate business as society will permit or force to flourish there—and the suburbanized keepers paid by society to keep the Indian reservation in order and off its conscience. Such is the ideal type of the drift course of the older city and suburb. We may well ask whether there is a homeostatic mechanism still extant that will of itself prevent the scenario here layed out. Is there a politics that will change the existing public-choice mechanism to one more likely to produce a better outcome?

4

Local Bourgeois Democracy: Government without Community?

JAMES Q. WILSON of Harvard, one of the country's foremost students of urban affairs, has described some of our larger and older central cities as "becoming the urban equivalent of Indian reservations on which perpetual wards of the state are subsidized by a system of 'welfare colonialism' that creates some serious problems (e.g., subsidizing broken homes) while solving others (e.g., preventing starvation)." In the same paper in which he made this statement Wilson also said something seemingly violently at odds with this, though perhaps not, namely, that

The most obvious indicators of the quality of life in our cities— per capita income, median school years completed, home ownership, morbidity rates, participation in cultural activities—are not much affected by the form or function of city government. . . . It would be hard to sustain the argument that the distribution of those things *most* important to *most* people is greatly affected by the distribution of power in the community.[1]

Yet if Wilson is right in his first assertion, as I think he is, that some of our older central cities are in a good way to becoming Indian reservations, this is of consequence. And if the form and functioning of city government significantly contribute to this outcome, who governs locally and how they govern may indeed be consequential.

Because whatever happens to people has to happen in space and because the cities are highly populous sites, they are at least the scenes of important action. As Roland Warren points out, though it is true that the vertical organizations of the nation-state and its bureaucracies, the states, the national unions, the national corporations, the professions, and the market have all eroded the autonomy of the local community, it is also true that all these vertical organizations must rely on the local horizontal organizations of the community for the local order on which they all must depend. Men live and die in Mississippi and on the docks of New Jersey because of the quality of local order. For them this fact is far from inconsequential.

Indeed, the presumed unimportance of the form and functioning of local government depends on who is involved and on his circumstances. For some, especially among the lower classes, the inconsequentiality of their local government is fraught with heavy consequences both for them and for their families. A trivial government, as some in Latin America, is a far from trivial thing for those whom that triviality deprives of a necessary instrument for bettering their condition.

In his classic study of government in New Haven Robert Dahl takes it for granted that, in spite of a steeply pyramidal distribution of income and a low standard of living, the lower classes of New Haven should give no thought to using politics as a means of altering their condition. But even if the failure of the working class to turn to local politics as a means of improving their lot were based on a sound political science perspective that acquainted them with the futility of engaging in it as other than a spectator sport, it would still be interesting to know how they had come to such a conclusion.

Many a newcomer, coming from a peasant culture such as southern Italy, would see the state from the perspective shown in *Christ Stopped at Eboli*,[2] as a hostile force that taxed the harvests, took sons for the army, and gave nothing in return. The American state and its visible embodiment, the city, might seem a great improvement, not because it did much but because it left him with more of what could be made in a prosperous society. The apathy toward local government on the part of the lower classes has not been the result of a conviction of the triviality of city hall—witness the expression, "you can't beat city hall" —but a feeling that the best you could hope for was to be let alone or, if lucky, to make something personally out of an "in" with the bosses. Government, as peasants knew it, was the possession of the upper class, used in the meager economies whence they came for their enrichment. The bitterness of the politics they knew, among the few that played at it, was owing to the real impoverishment of the "outs" in a society where government connection meant the difference between upper-class status and penury. This is the source of the private-regarding ethic ascribed to the immigrant peasants. The public-regarding alternative was something they had never seen.

Similarly, the political experience of workingmen was drawn from the struggles between employers and employees over jobs, wages, and working conditions. And that experience taught few lessons of a city or its upper-class rulers following a neutral conception of the public interest in its use of the police in strikes.

When the organized elements of the working class did gain enough political power to place their fellows in office, the explebes whom Dahl describes in *Who Governs?* they had learned a lesson from their business predecessors in power. The franchise politics of the utilities that Lincoln Steffens made memorable were a lesson in the use of the city as a device of self-enrichment. Unfortunately for the welfare of the lower class, the struggle to control the city, particularly the police, did not lead to any enduring well-considered attempt to use the city for lower-class welfare. In fact, when whatever sympathy there had been for socialist ideas before World War I was withered by the strong wave of anti-red hysteria following it, the construction trades were left in virtual possession of the field. But their business unionism had little concern for lower-class welfare, increasingly less class identification, and a growing sense of competitive but substantive identity with the interests of contractors and industry. The Gompers A.F. of L., suspicious of the state and desiring to have no rival competing for the workingman's allegiance, was riding high. Labor was as or more laissez-faire than business. The building code is a good symbol of the alliance of the construction trades and contractors in the exploitation of the city and its inhabitants. In fact, its putative concern for the protection of the public interest is a commentary on the perils of operationalizing this much abused abstraction. Construction trades and contractors can use the rhetoric of public-regarding virtue as well as the rest of us.

Not until the Great Depression brought back a wave of ideological unionism did there develop any significant interest in the city as a major device for promoting the welfare of the lower class.

Before then, ever since the triumph of the nation-state and the decay of municipal mercantilism, the dominant ideology was laissez-faire liberalism and the nightwatchman state. The role of the city was to provide such housekeeping services as could not be conveniently supplied by the private market. The city was primarily a device to teach the lower classes to play a responsible role in local government while leaving more important affairs to their social betters. The lessons were those of a deferential democracy and perhaps primarily to teach the representatives of the working class the value of money through the experience of spending some of their own in local government.

The English refer to local government as "sewerage without tears," an expression that indicates that for them as for us the problem of waste disposal has not always been tearless. But the reference is clearly to a workaday though necessary affair whose satisfactory functioning requires no more than routine competence and honesty. This same conception of local government is enshrined in the oft-repeated slogan of American municipal reform, that there is no Democratic or Republican way to pave a street. In the older rhetoric of the economy and efficiency advocates of the model charter, the city manager and the "good government" kit there was indeed only the "one best way" susceptible of scientific determination by municipal Platonists. Today, after arduous and inconclusive search by Ridley, Simon, and a host of eager devotees of a science of administration, this ideal has faded into the more humble aspiration of a way that would "satisfice." The early conception of the nineteenth-century city was one of public works, roads, bridges, waterworks, sewers, and public health. These latter were certainly of no small moment. Pure water and sewerage probably did more to lower the death rate than any public policies undertaken at national or state levels before or since.

But apart from public health and transport, two of government's main functions in any underdeveloped and developing country, the cities in the United States, unlike those in England and Europe, did little for the welfare of their people. (Though it should be noted that Croker and Tammany Hall devoted public funds to the Metropolitan Museum.) Education preceded bathhouse socialism. Sewerage, water, and transportation were common necessities of the whole society. Another function of local government was more controversial, posing a potential threat to the existing distribution of political and economic power. Throughout a considerable part of the nineteenth century, education and the extension of the franchise were both feared, since the classical liberals of that day could scarcely conceive that an educated, politically empowered poor would remain content with a bourgeois democracy.

The pressure for the greatest potential public good to be

enjoyed by the city's inhabitants was in education. Organized labor and workingmen's movements fought hard
against reluctant upper classes to bring about free public
education. Many conservatives were fearful that a lower
class that had learned to read would get above itself and
make trouble. But others felt that, once given the ballot,
the lower-class needs must be educated or they would indeed be dangerous. Education became a means for the political socialization of the foreign immigrant and the lower
class as well. Therefore, around the turn of the century,
when the representatives of W.A.S.P. middle-class culture
began to abandon control of city offices to the explebes, as
Dahl relates of New Haven and as occurred elsewhere at
the same time and for similar causes, they did not abandon
control of the local school boards. Indeed, until recently
this has been one of the few positions in the city on whose
overt control the better element has insisted. Like Plato,
with a surer instinct than political science, they knew in
their bones the importance of education.

Lord Bryce, in his *American Commonwealth*, refers to
the American city as the outstanding failure of an otherwise notable success in the practice of democracy. Seth
Low, whose experience as a mayor of New York (if not as
a president of Columbia University) might entitle him to
some respect, entered a dissent buttressed by more thought
and possibly knowledge than Bryce possessed. But the ver-
dict of opinion has gone to Bryce. His framing of the deficiencies of American local government taken from a British
perspective of Mill, sewerage without tears and bathhouse
socialism, has until recently colored much of our understanding of the civic condition and its ills, which he defined as dishonesty, graft, corruption, incompetence and
"good men" who "did not care." [3] According to this view,
public-regarding men of education, affluence, family (perhaps), and competence could readily ascertain public inter-

est in local government and honestly and competently carry it out. Or where they lacked expertise then they could hire the relevant experts in education, engineering, and other specialties to carry on the city's business in a businesslike fashion. The war cry of reform—which has echoed down the years and been espoused by right, left, and center—has been, in practice if not in rhetoric, "All power to the experts." Honest, well-intentioned amateurs band together to drive out the forces of organized plunder, corruption, incompetence, and partisan politics and replace their rule with the benign efforts of civil service—recruited experts.

This is the folklore of American municipal politics. All sectors of "informed opinion"—the press, the women's clubs, the bureaus of government research, enlightened businessmen, even enlightened labor leaders—accept almost without question the proposition that the doctor knows best and the only problem is to make sure of getting a doctor rather than a quack or a crook. This politics-less concentration on input with no capacity for or effective concern with the measurement of output has been costly. With the best of intentions the press, the good-government people, the enlightened businessmen, the unions, and informed opinion has turned the real business of the cities over to public bureaucracies selected and defended by civil service commissions, which they own and which have both an expert and a labor union claim to monopolize the work and the evaluation of the jurisdictions.

In practice this has meant that no matter who won at the polls the likelihood was that things would remain much the same. A patronage-minded city administration in Chicago that required political clearance of prospective teachers might be replaced by the enlightened machine of a Richard Daley and the schools turned over to a blue ribbon school board chosen from among the professionals, civic leaders, and other notables. Yet, in practice, what this has meant to the educational output of the system is largely unknown. The alliance between university schools of education, school systems, state boards of education, certifying organizations, teacher associations, the press, civic leadership, P.T.A.'s, and the whole closed corporation of education has successfully prevented any effective outside attempt to evaluate the system's cost effectiveness or, more broadly, success in improving the lives of either its pupils or those who were paying for it.

To be sure, education has been the favorite target and whipping boy of critics and reformers as diverse as Conant, Koerner, and Kozol, to name but three. But the attacks have never been couched in such a way as to raise the issue of what education was trying to do, what its measurable performance should strive to be, and how that performance would relate to the performance of the adult society. Education has been a self-justifying merit good in the hands of its own experts and a co-opted alliance of interests and amateurs who, for a variety of reasons, found the field of education a vocation and avocation.

What is true of education is to a degree also true of police, fire, health, and recreation. In all these services, as Dahl notes, there is a special coterie of individuals and interests that cluster about a public bureaucracy and serve in its management, criticism, and defense. It is only when an issue arouses the degree of passionate involvement of integration in the schools that a mayor such as Richard Daley is forced to move publicly into the closed arena of education. Politicians, media, and civic leaders have for varying reasons found political rewards in the apolitical politics of appearing to rely—and for most of the time actually relying—on the experts. The university-based schools of education, like the professional critics of the public bureaucracies, have a long-term customer-client relation with the school systems. Though they need to be sufficiently critical to maintain the credibility of their good housekeeping seals of approval, their criticism is from within and is made with the knowledge that both sides must do business together and that both are in fact jointly responsible for the existing state of affairs. When Benjamin Willis, Chicago's school superintendent, was under heavy attack by outraged blacks, deans of education were ready with their testimony. Chicago's burglars in blue unwittingly transferred Berkeley's dean of police administration, O. W. Wilson, from California to Illinois, where his city manager text became the reading for those to be reformed.

As James Q. Wilson's fascinating comparative study of police departments suggests,[4] the major difference one is apt to find is in smartness of uniforms and manners, the giving of tickets (and the ability to get them fixed), and the use of modern equipment and management devices. These differences do not appear to show any profound relation to variations in the incidence of major crimes. Perhaps no one expects them to and perhaps no one should. They may be a social placebo which, as long as it calms the nerves, is, like any other tranquilizer, worth its cost. One suspects, however, that the lower- and working-class population, which, unlike the middle class, suffers considerably from the incidence of violent crime, would hope for more than a placebo from society's investment. But as the Wilson study shows and as Norval Morris's figures and remarks indicate, those who have studied the matter find little evidence of any careful attempt to determine the impact of various amounts and types of police investment on the incidence of the various kinds of serious crime. The subject is as unresearched as the efficacity of patent medicines and probably for the same reasons. Why confuse the public if they have come to identify your activity with the thing they are afraid of and the result they hope to achieve? At present there are few departments—police, fire, education, or health—in which the reward system is so structured as to make it worth the management's while to seriously investigate the effectiveness of its measures.

One might have hoped that the thrust toward city planning would lead to an institutionalized center of staff work that would assess both individual departmental cost effectiveness and the combined effect of all city investments in achieving a set of coordinated goals designed to maintain and enhance the livelihoods of the city's people. This, of course, has not happened. The victim of its origins and history, city planning was always stamped with a beaux arts and architectural past. Its rationale has been the well-nigh —at least now, though still not in Jefferson County, Missouri—acceptance of the locality's right to protect a residence from the erection of a glue factory next door. The glue factory is a rather useful image, because though it seems to represent something universally recognized as undesirable, symbolically and actually it does not. What it does represent is an upper- and middle-class orientation toward planning as a means of protecting *their* amenities. Lower-class people have often preferred the stink and smoke of glue factories and iron foundries to lack of nearby employment.

But city planning was more concerned with the city beautiful than the city employable. Even today it is a rare planning commission that has even one economist on its staff. Concern for the city's economy devolves largely, if on anyone, on the Chamber of Commerce and the local public utility. Membership on the planning commission is likely to be another one of the appointive niches for the notables who choose to serve in posts that do not involve the politics of elections. Planning becomes part of another expediential alliance like education, self-enclosed and normally outside the political hurly-burly supported by press and civic leaders alike as another merit good to be produced and criticized by the experts.

Alan Altschuler's study of planning in one of the nation's supposedly more advanced cities, Minneapolis,[5] is a classic on the myth of master planning, the expediential concerns of the power structure, and the difficulty of so weakly based an operation as that of a planner to convert the mystique of the master plan into the embodiment of a rational well-grounded action program. Planning became a curious war against spot zoning and a defense of open space and monuments. Where, in the case of the highway engineers, planning had political muscle and money its plans tended to get realized however they conflicted with over-all plans. Robert Moses and the Port Authority in New York and Callahan and the Turnpike Commission in Massachusetts in varying ways reflect the honor society accords to men "who get things done" and the way, as things are, men get things done. The most effective politics in the city has been brick and mortar politics. It has not mattered much whether you were a saint or a sinner, a protagonist of ethnic politics and spoils as Curley and Callahan in Massachusetts were supposed to be or the cynosures of "good government" as Robert Moses and Austin Tobin of the Port Authority were at one time considered. As Robert Weaver and Robert Wood discovered when they tried to shift H.U.D. from a well-nigh exclusive concern with physical structure to what they seemed to think was needed, a concern with social structure, brick and mortar is organized labor and capital and pays the political bills. A competing rival base of power is difficult to come by.

It has not been just poor sociology that has caused the nation to concentrate on housing as a means to the alleviation of the condition of the poor, though sociology doubtless helped disarm the judicial conscience in lending the power of eminent domain to urban renewal as an appropriate exercise of the police power. And to be sure it was convenient for the press and middle-class liberals to make urban renewal a species of white (or white man's) magic that would cure all the associated ills of the slum—crime, ill health, poor educational and job motivation, and the rest. Only yesterday the Americans for Democratic Action and other impeccable liberal forces considered urban renewal the sovereign remedy for the city's ills. In this they joined some strange bedfellows whose opposition to public housing was inveterate and whose sudden interest in government intervention in housing was strangely inconsistent with their opposition to the welfare state elsewhere. In the name of removing slums and housing the poor the nation spent billions to, in effect, reduce the housing available to the poor and drive up the price of what remained. The massive displacements in Millcreek in Saint Louis and elsewhere were accomplished to the applause of the press and all right thinking elements. Though their damage to the city and the poor has been incalculable no Pentagon papers have appeared to cause a reassessment. As James Wilson has remarked, such critics as Charles Abrams, Herbert Gans, Chester Hartman, and Marc Fried were unhonored; only when President Johnson made similar criticism after mounting public outcry did it become official.

During the 1950's the miracle of New Haven, Mayor Lee, and a new breed of mayors elsewhere were seen as revitalizing the cities. New Haven literally became the Moscow subway of conventional liberalism. Yet the new convergence of power depicted by Robert Salisbury,[6] in which the enlightened mayor-politician rallies downtown interests, mobilizes the experts of the universities, and receives the backing of the press, the enthusiastic support of the construction trades, the admiration of the voters, and funds from the federal treasury has lost momentum during the 1970's. Of the new breed, as Lyle Fitch remarks, only

Daley survives, the mayor who successfully combined the office with a functioning and effective machine. One might have thought that the combination of business, labor, the universities, and a trained set of experts, such as New Haven's West Point of urban renewal, would have developed a self-correcting theory of the city and its problems. In the event, the most successful of the urban renewers were a set of public-enterprise Zeckendorffs, some it is true, far more fortunate and enduring than that Icarus of private enterprise. But they were men of action, impatient with theory and impatient with research designs and evaluation. In this they were no different from most government and most business for that matter, though one might have hoped that the academic connection might have made a difference. We still await a study of New Haven, not one that deals with Mayor Lee as minor league prince in the writing of some political science Machiavelli, but one that tells us what the millions spent achieved, for good or ill, in the lives of the people of New Haven. Martin Anderson's "The Federal Bulldozer" [7] remains without adequate answer or alternative critical assessment of facts that now should be better known. We are the poorer, not for the money spent but for the lessons unlearned.

William Slayton, Urban Renewal Commissioner of the old Housing and Home Finance Agency, has tried to draw some lessons from years spent in the enterprise:

If I were to identify a single basic element of naïveté in the original formulation of the program, I would stress the absence of the concept of a city-wide long term strategy. . . . A real estate operation regardless of scale and sponsorship, is not going to do the job of restructuring our cities. Some large part of the problem in the cities rests in the failure to resolve the problems of those in the population too impoverished to afford decent housing or a decent standard of life. Some large part of the problem rests in the limitations on members of minority groups in terms of both housing and job opportunities. Some large part

of the problem rests on the absence of the vigorous local economy necessary to provide employment opportunities and alternatives to its population. Our ultimate need is for action which
deals with all of these problems. We are past the point where
the physical planning of the community was enough. We now
need at the community level an integrated process of physical
planning, social planning and economic planning.[8]

Slayton, at least, after years and billions spent, came to
recognize that brick and mortar by itself would not do the
job, that the needs of a community as a functioning whole
had to be met. Yet how to make a society whose production organizations are highly specialized and oriented toward and coordinated by the (frequently national) market
responsive to the pattern of needs of a local community
that is frequently low on funds remains as a major unsolved
problem.

Ostensibly, the urban renewal program attempted to provide decent housing for the poor and remove slums, or so
it was thought. But as Scott Greer has pointed out, Congress required that the program rely on the private sector
for its implementation; thus if the program were to succeed, it had to yield a profit to the various segments of the
housing industry. Not surprisingly, what ensued was the
search for those spots where renewal could remove structures, assemble land, and provide the opportunity for some
one to build at a profit. Given the high costs of construction, this generally meant what was euphemistically called
middle-income housing, often luxury high-rise apartments,
and, increasingly, central-city office buildings. Though not
cynical in intent, the program operated in the name of
housing the poor to unhouse the poor and the black and to
rehouse banks and other downtown businesses. Had this
been a direct program of government subsidy for business
and the middle class it would scarcely have been politically feasible. Had it been even claimed seriously that this

assistance to the middle class and the central business district would in some clearly demonstrable way favorably alter the condition of the poor the program could have been examined on its merits to determine whether it was indeed calculated to have any such effect. Though some such rationales were cooked up after the fact they were never made the serious basis of the program.

The lesson we have yet to learn from the nation's housing program is the need for a politics, liberal or conservative, that implements its abstractions in programs clearly and measurably designed to change dimensions of specifiable observable people in specifiable ways. It would have been helpful if the Democratic Club movement in New York, the Americans for Democratic Action, the Independent Voters of Illinois, the Young Conservatives, and others who have dabbled in the politics of the city could make clear to themselves in just what ways they proposed that the action of government affect particular people's lives. If these people were clearly self-interested as a pressure group they might have a check on the efficacity of their programs through their own consciousness of the programs' results for them. But since they may entertain a public-regarding concern and hence have no particular observable public in mind, good intentions plus the advice of the experts seem to suffice. Since the experts, be they police, educators, housers, or doctors, are for the most part locked into the ongoing existing institutional structure, public policy will likely purchase more of the same but under a new name.

For the most part the politics of the city is conducted not for the sake of its inhabitants but for the material and ideal rewards of nonresidents or those whose income insulates them against the city's hardships. The material interests do provide some reality control. Unions, contractors, banks and so on, though sometimes momentarily carried away, know whether their material concerns prosper. The ideologically motivated, however, have virtually no feedback as to the efficacity of their good intentions; except in a rare case like that of Slayton, they move from program to program and nostrum to nostrum. The middle class and the media can afford a politics of fad and slogans, since if worst comes to worst they can buy their way. In fact, because by and large they can buy their way they indulge in a politics of purchased solutions and suppose that these solutions are there to buy if you can only rustle up the money. The problem of making the solutions is quite another matter.

Medicare is a magnificent example of the politics of purchased solutions—and of how billions can be spent through a health industry with only deteriorating services and inflation to show as a result. It seems so easy to put money in people's hands to buy a merit good such as health and expect one's good intentions to be rewarded. What happens is quite another story. With the Reuther and Kennedy plans as unwilling as the American Medical Association to tackle the health delivery system, there is little reason to expect anything but a continuance of inflation. Existing proposals fail even to come to grips with whether the existing health care system is providing health or has many other objectives such as teaching doctors, studying interesting diseases, or much less edifying ends.

In New York City, the country's leading experiment was undertaken with a minimum of public consultation in a way that sheds light on how in the most democratic of our local democracies what concerns people's lives can be decided without their consent or even their opinion being asked. New York hospitals were put under a hospital corporation following the recommendations of the Piel Commission after a perfunctory hearing by the city council and an even more perfunctory one by the state legislature.

With Gerard Piel and Eveline Burns the only two outsiders from the health establishment (save the bankers who are in some ways a veto group), the Piel Commission was a typically blue ribbon affair. With the medical schools, the voluntary hospitals, the city's budget director and *The New York Times* supporting the commission's plan, an apparently reluctant mayor under pressure from Albany agreed. Everybody in the health establishment, including its bankers, had a voice in the decision. Even Gotbaum and his union, the only likely voice for the users of the public hospitals, was involved. It seemed to go virtually without saying that a decision affecting the lives of New York citizens should be made without consulting them. Whereas blue ribbon civic leadership, bankers, the union, the bureaucracies, and the press all had standing to be considered, the patients of the hospitals and the population from which they came had to rely on the city council, the mayor, and their supposed virtual representation through the public members of the blue ribbon panel. At the hearing before the city council the affected population did make itself heard, was concerned, and received the concession of advisory boards that might or might not be significant.

The case of the New York City hospital corporation is an excellent example of the nontrivial nature of local politics. Health care can be a matter of life and death and quite frequently does spell the difference between ill health and poverty or the capacity to earn a decent living. The assumption that the interests of the patients and the relevant populations would be automatically taken care of by the prestigious members of a blue ribbon board, the doctors, the administrators of the voluntary hospitals, the employee union leader, and that part of the formal political process involved has been gravely questioned. The users of the public hospitals were unrepresented either by experts of their own or, like the employees, though these but recently, by a union of their own. Nor does the political process seem to have been in any position to act as an effective protagonist.

The Office of Economic Opportunity in giving vogue to the slogan "maximum feasible participation of the poor" was not just paying lipservice to a fashionable academic phrase. The areas such as housing, health, and education, programs ostensibly in the interests of the poor (and the not so poor) fail to achieve publicly stated goals. A public-choice theorist would look at the mechanism of incentives and seek to understand the reasons behind the unintended outcome. Why does the system reward behavior other than that leading to the results it claims to desire? One answer comes loud and clear: If the system is designed to respond to cash, him who has gits. Even public programs such as housing, health, and education are responsive to differences of income in the population. Housing goals were to be achieved through the private sector. The private sector responds to effective demand. Education, though in the public sector, responds to the income of the population it serves and the higher income populations have been able to segregate their demand through suburban schools. Health, through the two-class hospital system and the fee-for-service system, responds like housing to effective demand. Not only is there a problem of difference of effective demand for the goods allocated in the private sector but there is a problem of making the lower-class demand effective in the public sector for public goods ostensibly produced in its behalf.

The problem of effective local democracy is twofold: power and cognitive competence. The poor performance of the New York public school system, pictured to be a remote, inflexible bureaucracy, may suggest to the Ford Foundation and the Harvard School of Education, among others, decentralization to Ocean Hill-Brownsville. Some social science research strongly suggests that students with involved parents do better, and power over the school could be the price of parental identification and concern. But others, including the teachers' union, may well say, "What do these parents know about running a school?" Irving Kristol quite appropriately asks, "Decentralization for What?" [9] The answer to that question is an old one. Lord Lindsay gave it the appropriately humble Socratic touch by insisting on the capacity of the wearer to know when the shoe pinches. Perhaps one might insist on the decentralization having a recognizable shoe fitting on a determinate body of people who might usefully tell the experts it pinched. Conceivably they might even usefully tell them more than that.

Christopher Jencks and some others have suggested giving the poor, and possibly the not so poor, money or script with which to purchase education for their children. [10] This is to take the mode of the affluent and attempt for a limited purpose to assimilate the poor to them. Some such notion was behind Medicare. Yet it seems unlikely that lower-income people can be given equality with upper-income people in the purchase of a valued item, certainly not without radically altering the condition of supply. But Jencks's suggestion has its appeal, though not, it would appear, to Mr. Shanker and the teachers' union.

But even with money, one needs knowledge to choose. The economists' market assumption of perfect knowledge among buyers and sellers assumes away one of our most difficult problems. Even the middle class can spend its money on wasteful patent medicines and a health care that may not be much better. The market system assumes the development of increasing knowledge and its fruitful application through the forces of competition. A rather unlikely restructuring of the existing health industry would be necessary to bring about anything near the conditions the economists posit for a competitive market. Under existing conditions there is little reason to expect the likely outcomes of the existing set of incentives in the health industry to result in actions leading to quality health care for all but exceptional members of the lower class, and certainly not for lower-class communities considered as a whole. As Dr. Willoughby Lathem, deputy director of the biomedical sciences division of the Rockefeller Foundation, writes,

> To hear the anguished voices, both public and private, now abroad in the land one would think that the current problem was principally an economic one. It is not. The progressive escalation in the cost of medical care is, of course, of great concern, and ranks as a problem demanding attention and, if possible, resolution. But it is not the primary difficulty. The fundamental need is reorganization of the system, not because it is expensive but because it is inadequate and inequitable.[11]

What Dr. Lathem and others in the field of community medicine maintain is that a health care system that centers on the hospital with little knowledge or concern for the patient before he enters or after he leaves is hopelessly inadequate. It is even scientifically impoverished in its divorce from data needed to understand the phenomena with which it should be concerned. One of the fruits of the War on Poverty and the Office of Economic Opportunity has been to assist in the movement leading to departments of community medicine in leading medical schools. These departments represent an interesting reversal in the tendency of clinical medicine to concentrate almost exclusively on the individual. By conceiving of the comprehensive health needs of an area, a variety of factors impinging on health can be considered by a team that assumes responsibility for the health of a neighborhood. Such a community health team practicing community medicine is the counterpart of the neighborhood community organization that resembles a consumers' health cooperative. The models of the under-developed countries have more to offer the people of the city, not just because they, like the people of the city, lack money but because their models are more cost effective than our own. The suggestion has been made that the mid-dle-class cooperatives of Los Angeles County that adopt the Lakewood Plan are strong buyers since they purchase their public goods through city manager purchasing agents who know the merchandise and can drive a hard bargain for the goods they require. The people of the city are even more in need of public goods cooperatives manned by competent purchasing agents in their corner to see that they get their money's worth and their votes' worth in the services the city does, and might be made to, provide.

The health field is in many ways typical of the strains in the society. As Eliot Freidson maintains, "The medical profession exercises a degree of control over the delivery of health services that precludes both effective and adequate health care for the majority of the client population." [12] According to Freidson, the solution will require the in-volvement of clients in decision-making and the setting of standards, even though this is opposed by the doctors on the grounds of professionalism, the need to make decisions in a complex and nonpublicly verifiable way for which they are accountable to no one except their peers. The doctor's assumed capacity to determine pathology—who is sick and what is health—is central to his authority in the struc-ture. Freidson says,

The problem arises, however, when outsiders may no longer evaluate the doctor's work by the rules of logic and the knowl-edge available to all educated men, and when the only legiti-mate spokesman on an issue relevant to all men must be some-one who is officially certified. This is the central policy issue in the provision of such personal services as health care, an issue underlying such concrete questions as how the services are to be paid for and how they are to be presented to the public. The issue is who is to determine what the goals of the service are and the concrete models by which its goals are to be pursued. Accountability for effective and humane services must in some way be more responsive to the lay client himself.[13]

The poor, lacking the money to make such a demand through the market, must make it through politics if they make it at all.

Organizing people to, in a sense, empower them could be for the community medicine doctor just another form of community development. Only through such a development is the preventive and environmental medicine so necessary for the poor likely to come within their resources. (Though we may find that what is good for Watts may be good for Beverley Hills too.) However unwillingly, the medical industry is pioneering in community medicine and bringing local people into an effective twoway relation with the medical experts, thereby subjecting the formerly authoritarian hierarchy to at least a dash of participatory democracy.

It is also, because of its labor shortage, involved in creating new careers for the poor. As the poorest paid sectors of public and private employment, the hospitals are plagued with a chronic shortage of staff. Much of the staff are poor and black. It has occurred to a number of hospital administrators that their manpower shortage could be overcome by making use of and upgrading employees at the aide and orderly level. There are, of course, real problems in doing this. Professionals feel threatened. No field is as deeply entrenched and enmeshed in licensure as the health industry. Some twenty-five health occupations are now licensed and the number of state licensing bodies runs in the hundreds. Many licensing requirements not only call for the passing of a written examination but prescribe evidence of training at an accredited institution.

All this makes the job difficult, but the need is pressing. Dr. James Houghton, first deputy administrator of the New York City hospital department, testifying before the poverty subcommittee of the Senate labor committee as to the critical need for nurses, has observed that "if we took our own employees, people who were mature, people with families, who are already working for us, if we as an agency create the opportunities for them to upgrade their professional skills, perhaps that will engender the kind of loyalty that will make them stay with us in the system." [14]

Certainly, the experience of the navy in giving a basic sixteen-week course for corpsmen, an advanced training program of twenty weeks, and a wide range of specialties in periods ranging from seven to sixty weeks has made people wonder about present licensing requirements. Experience with the program has led Sumner Rosen to conclude that "Prolonged and segmented training sequences for civilian health occupations are particularly difficult to justify, particularly when there are very few cases in which basic training in a special area receives any recognition when one wishes to move to a more advanced level."

Thanks to Vietnam, the poor and the black are becoming aware of what the armed forces have been able to do. They become increasingly impatient with, on the one hand, being denied medical care in their neighborhoods and, on the other, being confined to the most menial hospital jobs by a licensure system they regard as irrelevant. New York City has established an upgrading program for licensed practical nurse to registered nurse. Taken together with the nurse's aide upgrading program designed by District Council 37 of the American Federation of State and County Employees and supported by the Departments of Labor and Health, Education and Welfare, this creates, at least in principle, a career ladder in nursing in this major hospital system. The city, albeit not of conscious and set purpose, and in halting fashion, has thus begun to develop its people so they can surmount the barriers to their own employment and help themselves through helping one another. Health, as one of the nation's top growth industries and a labor-intensive industry in the bargain, is of concern to the city's people as a service they need and a service in which they can be employed and even have careers.

The politics of the city could be highly consequential for its inhabitants. Indeed, it is just that for those who gain from the projects it undertakes, such as urban renewal, highways, mass transit, and the operation of its hospitals and other services. But though the city is normally thought of in the economic literature as redistributive, there is reason to doubt that most of its inhabitants benefit to the degree supposed from its programs. Certainly many show scant gratitude for what they receive and little profit into the bargain. Though Saint Louis spends heavily on the city's hospitals, the infant mortality rate in 1971 [15] was one-third greater than that of Hong Kong in 1965.[16] Lead poisoning is pandemic among children in the thousands of dilapidated houses whose ceilings and walls are peeling. Who then is really served by the city's hospital expenditures? Does university control of hospitals ensure the most efficient service of the health needs of the inhabitants of the city or the teaching needs of the universities' medical schools and the research interests of their staffs?

The priorities on a health problem such as lead poisoning provide an objective test of what the system in being regards as important, responds to, and indeed can respond to. In the number of people affected and in the consequences of the affliction for the victims and their families lead poisoning is anything but trivial. It is even nontrivial to the larger society in the price it too must ultimately pay. But the going system treats the problem in its current calculus as trivial. It is not that information about the existence of widespread lead poisoning and its danger is suppressed. The press and television have given it almost as much and as sympathetic coverage as the slaughter of the baby seals in the Gulf of Saint Lawrence. Meetings have been held even in the halls of the medical association. Slumlords have been denounced. Municipal ordinances have been passed that, if enforced, would eject on to the street the tenants they were designed to help. The city's building department, investigating for lead poisoning violations, finds other violations. The property owner, faced with repair costs ruinously in excess of his rents, threatens to, and frequently does, abandon his building, leaving the protected tenant homeless and the city with one more soon-to-be-vandalized hulk. Strapped for funds, the city awaits aid from Washington, which in its current stringency finds lead poisoning not one of its higher priorities.

And so it goes. Some say, burn the properties down. But where will the people live? Others note that many families who live in housing subject to lead hazards still seem able to keep their children from eating paint and plaster. As the going system operates, denunciation of villains will accompany the search for outside funds. Efforts to modify the behavior of families to prevent their children's ingesting lead will remain undeveloped, even unexplored either because this unheavenly aspect of the city is regarded, as it is by some, as a fatal human weakness or, in the case of others, as a weakness that can only be remedied by making damaging admissions that would be a blow to the cause.

The case typifies the problem of the city and its politics. Liberals concerned with a cause and with bad housing are anxious not to divert attention from the goal of replacing the substandard housing in which the people live. Politically it is expedient to pillory the present property owners regardless of the economics of the situation. The remedy, insofar as it gets beyond the city code and its enforcement, a device that cannot be taken seriously since it only leads to further property abandonment, moves directly to the state and, far more likely, to Washington. What is in the city's power is either deemed impossible, politically inexpedient, or not worth doing. Modification of the behavior of families that do not protect their children as others similarly circumstanced clearly do, is not attempted. Black militants find it hard to admit both that blame lies on both sides and that a degree of individual responsibility, and therefore freedom, does exist. Privately, like Malcolm X, one might urge family pride and self-help. Publicly the position has to be one of denouncing those guilty of profiting from the poisoning of innocent children and a denial of the slander on some of one's people that facing their parental failure might encourage.

Political leaders, press, unions, doctors all see the most ready remedy for the problem in Washington. Federal funds enable the purchase of solutions to local problems— or seem to. With funds one can purchase the cooperation that one's political powers of persuasion find difficult to attain. With funds one can create human development corporations, pay salaries, buy materials—all without any major local political effort or change. Our experience with foreign aid should have taught us that such aid, if unaccompanied by the local capacity to put it to effective use, goes almost inevitably to support the status quo. The failure to make a major effort to change the behavior of the families who could but do not care enough and know enough to do what is in their power to do to protect their children is emblematic of the city's politics and why it drifts toward becoming the trivial dispenser of funds received from other governments, trivial, that is, in what it does but by no means trivial by what people lose— because of its failure to do what it could do. The city becomes a larger order of the other-directed dependent enterprise Vidich and Bensman describe in the *Small Town in Mass Society*, [17] doing only those things that superior governments fund.

City inhabitants are in many ways the victims of a middle-class politics that fails to see that they are potential and actual assets of the city, who if they do not become assets will almost certainly become liabilities. As Greer and Minar remark of the city's attempt to regain the middle class, "The central city-suburb schisms turn urban renewal into a holy war to recapture the suburban, white, middle class—a war the central city is doomed to lose—and distract attention from the major clientele of the central city: the working class, the ethnics, the disprivileged." [18] In fact, Greer and Minar might have pointed out that the best strategy for bringing some of the middle class back to the city and holding others still there would be to make the city truly effective in the service of this neglected clientele and by doing so transform the city. A few thousand black and white young males account for most of the street crime that increasingly make city life seem intolerable. These few thousand constitute a major part of the drug problem. Their lack of suitable employment is one of the major sources of A.D.C., the rise of illegitimacy, the welfare family, and the intergenerational transmission of a culture of poverty. No really effective concerted attempt has been made to modify their behavior and the conditions giving rise to it. Their ethic of immediate gratification that makes the city unheavenly is, one hopes, not a fatally determined response. A city not itself fatalistic in its acquiescence would seek to understand the logic that presently entails this behavior and mount intervention strategies to accomplish its favorable alteration.

There are two kinds of responses (among many) that people may make to problems of the city. One, stressed by public-choice theorists and others, sees the individual as a chooser of public goods, with local governments as suppliers of a varying set of packages at different prices. In this analogy to the economic market, governments compete for customers and customers achieve their ends by discriminating and selective purchasing. Another response involves the person's attempting to produce rather than merely buy the public goods he requires. This response would see the city and its possibilities as a cooperative, even a cooperative embracing perhaps a set of neighborhood cooperatives including such special purpose activities as health cooperatives. This is the response of the man with limited money who makes the down payment on his house with sweat equity. Such a city would have to have leaders and staff who perceived both the possibility of energizing sweat equity among its citizens and how in practical reality the mobilizable sweat could be turned to good account. The middle-class response is deeply dependent on the purchase-ready mode of its wants and the purchase of expert advice for its received opinions.

The middle-class response, which by and large dominates the thinking of the city and its leaders, relies on purchase and the delegation of problem solution to the accredited experts. Well meant as it is, it debilitates the city, as it becomes increasingly expensive, depending, as it does, on the self-evaluation of the experts. The growth of highly specialized bureaucracies leads to self-contained guilds which monopolize their areas and, like trade unions, become more and more averse to any but their members performing functions that they have stamped as their own. The police want no private persons or private enterprises in policing. The teachers, despite protestations to the contrary, want no one else teaching reading, least of all do Mr. Shanker and the teachers' union want parents shopping around for the instruction of their children. The medical industry is so safely swaddled in licensure that the laity is fortunate to be able to bandage a finger without running the risk of the illegal practice of medicine. All this may produce the fruits of specialization that Adam Smith observed in his pin factory. It can also become an unbearable burden if the mounting costs of the specialized bureaucracies bear no fruit in increasing the efficiency of the city's economy, a goal which they neither accept for themselves nor have imposed on them by others. They lack any over-all scoring system—like a corporation's profit and loss account—from which citizens can determine what contribution if any they make to the common concern and whether the contribution repays the cost. Instead, they are treated as self-justifying merit goods, like so many works of art, to be judged by the experts and gaped at by the uninitiated general public.

The middle-class person can exercise some power over the situation by shopping around, and so, to a degree, can the stable working man. Both pay heavily for the cost ineffectiveness of their public goods, but they both have freedom to move, either where they think the quality of the public goods is better or at any rate the price is more in line with what they are prepared to afford. Those at the bottom of society's heap most desperately need public goods, health, education, police, job training, employment service, and the like that are cheap in terms both of their resources and of the resources available to the city and really serviceable to their needs. They quite literally cannot afford that the city's public goods be objects of conspicuous consumption in Veblen's sense with high honorificence and low utility. Nor can the city afford this either, though public goods as an art form are more likely to be criticized by their expert critics for their honorific than their utilitarian value. The city and the poor alike have or rather should have an interest in the viability of the city's economy. Both have a real if unperceived interest in the employability of the poor and in upgrading the employment of the poor. It is toward that end that public goods of education, health, security, housing, transport, and information should be structured. Of the poor, the tired cliche "If you are not part of the solution you are part of the problem" still speaks to the point.

If many of the inhabitants of the city can not be helped to become self-supporting (and city-supporting) members of the enterprise, if most of the city's public goods become ever more costly without contributing measurably to the viability of the city's economy, then the city will have to become more and more dependent on resources from without. Inevitably, if its local taxes go to support the dead weight of a dependent population and a set of economically unproductive public services, the remaining productive sector of the city's businesses and people that can will seek to escape the burden by moving elsewhere. Only those who have to or in the peculiar conditions of the dependent city make their profit by doing so will remain. The new specialization of the city, how it pays its way as Indian reservation, poor farm, specialized area for deviance, crime, and the uses the outside society can and will thrust on it become the drift course of the dependent city. The city and the outside society pay a price for this scenario. Unseen and out of the way in the reservation, the development of the central city will present far greater problems. The alternative to the dependent city is the city that turns its inhabitants from liabilities to themselves and the city into assets and its economy from disinvestment and decline to stability and growth.

In many ways the medical industry illustrates both the problems and the possibilities of the city. It is also quite typical of the problems and possibilities of other of the cities' public goods. The structure of interests that has evolved leads the practice of medicine, along with other enterprises, from the poor and the city to the affluent and the suburbs. The inadequate resources available to the public sector of the health industry lead to a rationing as demeaning and difficult as that of much of welfare. Indeed, much of the public sector purportedly for the poor is, as in the case of mental health, diverted to the middle-class practice of psychiatry. Recognition of the degree to which the existing structure fails to respond to the needs of the poor and even the nonpoor has grown of late. But responses such as Medicare, the typical tactic of attempting to buy a solution without altering either the supply or the existing delivery system, have led to inflation and disappointment. Successor programs, such as those currently under consideration, those of Senator Kennedy, the A.M.A. and the Administration for instance, bid fair to have similar results.

The health problems of the poor, however, have their hopeful side. Some of the medical profession are taking themselves to where the people live with profit to the people and to the practice of medicine. Concern for how most effectively to improve the health of a geographically defined population in this as in other public services yields a reality control that can produce a relevant scoring system, defensible priorities, and an informed appreciation of cost benefits. The departments of community medicine that have recently emerged are rediscovering preventive and environmental medicine. The discipline of concern with giving meaning to the efficient use of resources for a specific population within the constraints of limited resources and the given characteristics of the population produces similar effects and yields payoffs similar to those of the medical practices of the navy and other services. Though a logic such as that which requires a navy doctor to administer an anesthetic to the badly wounded and concentrate on restoring the lightly wounded to combat effectiveness in order to fight the ship or even save it is fortunately unnecessary, some logic of the situation and the people's needs is necessary. It is this that yields purpose, rationality, and intelligent concern where previously at best scientific curiosity and undirected compassion and at worst self-indulgence, wasteful extravagance, and "making it" held sway.

The situation of the poor of the city has, because of constraints akin to the naval situation, forced reconsideration of the necessity and the cost effectiveness of the existing health delivery system. Among other possibilities this school of necessity has raised the question of whether the poor could be used to treat the poor and whether the existing system of licensure is protecting the people's health or some of the people's jobs to the disadvantage of the rest. The experience of the navy and other services and the war in Vietnam with its stream of returning corpsmen have given the questions added point. The chronic manpower shortages of the hospitals have also compelled consideration of the upgrading of aides and orderlies. The manpower problems of the medical industry have proved to be opportunities to pioneer the transformation of the city's poor into a resource through which both the costs of medical care for the poor can be reduced and the barriers to the effective delivery of that care surmounted. The successful creation of training programs and career ladders in nursing in the New York City hospitals demonstrate what Ivar Berg has maintained, that the present educational credentialism unrelated to the realistic requirements of the job is dysfunctional to the utilization of presently wasted manpower and a hindrance to the people's self-support. For the city the discovery that its unutilized and underutilized population can be gainfully employed in the medical industry is one that could lead to similar consequences in other fields with incalculable benefit to the newly employed and the city alike. This is the gist of the manpower strategy Wilbur Thompson advocates in his urban economics.

Local Bourgeois Democracy

The medical industry, in opening new careers to the poor and bringing the existing system of authority and licensure into question, is beginning a crisis of legitimacy and order that is bound to prove painful to it and to others. Sumner Rosen notes,

The growing self awareness among new careerists and low income workers can alter both the internal climate and the external relationships of these systems, when management is sympathetic and sensitive and when it is not. Even when the professionals and system managers support the new-career principles, the course of events may well be swift, disturbing and ultimately destructive.[19]

Rosen calls attention to the disputes in 1968 at the Topeka, Kansas, State Hospital and the one in 1969 at the Lincoln Mental Health Service in New York City which, as he says, though differing in origin had remarkably similar results. These events are reminiscent of the sit-down strikes of the 1930's and their air of the tragicomedy of French Revolutionary amateur theatricals. The language of Emerson Stamps, chairman of the Kansas Health Workers, in a telegram seeking help in their work in takeover is revealing:

Our national precedent must be followed by all hospital workers in their struggle for dignity, participation and recognition. Because of moral position, because we care for our patients and the people of our state, because of the arrogance and political corruption that riddles our hospital system we have struck a significant blow for human liberation. Our issue is a community issue. We have support from all the people despite the lies and divisive reporting in our local press and T.V. all owned by one man.[20]

This telegram gives some sense that there is a jinni in the bottle and that all hell can break loose when it comes out. And there is no way in this or any other revolutionary change to be sure that the good guys will not catch it too. This much one has to grant the conservatives who denounce the folly of attempts to change the existing author-

153

ity structure and so face the turbulence of a destabilized social order.

The change in the existing authority structure oddly reminiscent of Mao's cultural revolution in both its populist rhetoric and its association of existing experts with mandarin exploitation, will necessitate an altered basis of authority. Such a new base must control not only the arrogance, aloofness, and unwillingness to serve people of the experts but that of the fervid Emerson Stamps and their cohorts as well. The self-constituted representatives of the people can become as domineering and arrogant when they are the aroused Kansas Health Workers questing for dignity and recognition as the medical establishment and unfortunately far more incompetent, whatever their good intentions. The need to develop an authority that founds itself on relevance to people's needs, concern for though not servile subservience to people's opinions, and an objective evaluation of performance on the basis of testable and improving criteria is taking shape in the term "accountability." Eliot Freidson puts his finger on it when he says,

The problem arises, however, when outsiders may no longer evaluate the doctor's work by the rules of logic and the knowledge available to all educated men, and when the only legitimate spokesman on an issue relevant to all men must be someone who is officially certified. . . . Accountability for effective and humane services must, in some way, be more responsive to the lay client himself.[21]

Making the service bureaucracies, experts, and employees responsible and accountable to their lay public is the job ahead. To do so the lay public must acquire both the rules of logic and a sufficiency of knowledge and the courage to use it.

As Robert Bish suggested of the upper-class cooperatives of the Lakewood Plan in Los Angeles County, one way is to have knowledgeable purchasing agents in one's corner and in some fashion to get arm's-length bargaining between those responsible for the production of services and those who need to consume them. Since the people of the central city and the older suburb are short of cash and lacking in the options cash provides, the model of the city they require may be less that of the posh Miami hotel that they can take or leave for another hotel than that of the city as a producers' and consumers' cooperative designed for humane use in which the citizens participate in both roles. Scott Greer and David Minar pose the question in the current context:

Today the boundaries of all local units are permeable: residents, stores, factories move with ease outside the city—carrying with them all sorts of resources for the municipal corporation. As this occurs some struggle to reconstitute the city state; it is a losing struggle, for the nation state guarantees freedom of movement, and nothing requires continued commitment. Thus, the question arises: Could we, or should we, try to reconstitute the older style of spatially defined community? [22]

5

A Possible Future:
The City as a
Humane Cooperative

THE UNWALLED CITY, open to all with none compelled to stay, must earn a loyalty it cannot require. Ideally, its citizens will be citizens of choice rather than compulsion; its walls will be the shared purposes its activities make possible. That is why the future of the city is as a humane cooperative directed to the improvement of the economic and social conditions of its members. Its appeal will be to those who need it, need it because they are poor and must pool their scant resources of money and labor to produce what they cannot purchase, because the productive possibilities of active citizenship are nowhere else so possible, and because the rich diversity of the city offers far more potential for creativity than the homogenized condition of the like circumstanced and like minded. The strength of the city is in its diversity, its varied appeal, capabilities, and activities; its decline has been accompanied by the homogenization into the city of old industry, old people, the poor, the discriminated against and their keepers.

The tragedy of the city has been its loss of purpose and self-direction. Above all, its rulers, despite frequent good will and strong attachments of sentiment, lack a permanent and reasoned commitment to its future. Often, while running the city, they no longer share much of its life. They neither expose their families and children to its streets and schools nor use its possibilities as other than a place of business. Wittingly and unwittingly, many city rulers exploit the city and its remaining inhabitants with public investments that are privately profitable but socially costly and wasteful. Fewer and fewer businesses remain to contribute to the city's economic base or otherwise see their future as bound up with that of the city. The city's service bureaucracies become more and more so much dead weight contributing little to the viability of the city's economy and weighing ever more heavily on its limited fiscal resources. Policemen, firemen, teachers, welfare workers come to see themselves as keepers, a class apart from the inhabitants.

The city then is run neither by nor for its inhabitants. Worst of all, many of the city's inhabitants are regarded as, and are, liabilities to themselves and the city. But the leaders of the city and its bureaucracy, instead of seriously attempting to change these liabilities into assets, make an excuse out of the condition and a business of managing human liabilities. The city's only resource is treated as no resource at all.

Yet if the people of the city are broke and stay broke the city will surely go broke too. In that case the only means of staying afloat is for those who run the city's bureaucracies to persuade the outside society to pay them to run the city as Indian reservation and poor farm. This is the present drift of events. Since the Great Society and the poverty programs, many efforts in a seemingly opposite direction have, it is felt, been made, and the pages of the press abound with stories of training programs sponsored by the federal government and efforts of organizations such as the National Alliance of Businessmen to employ the city's hard core. Sar Levitan and Garth Mangum, who have studied the subject in detail, have found few examples of other than public relations successes.[1] Mostly, the training has been conducted to employ the trainers rather than those they trained. Projects for employing the hard core have been at best motivated by well-intentioned benevolence, often by a desire to be in fashion and secure favorable publicity, and not infrequently, at worst, by a willingness to exploit the hard core and the taxpayers.

In almost all cases the weakness of such programs is that, except for the parasitic rackets, they do not stem from any perception of sustained opportunities for profitable employment of those to be trained. But if the city is not to become a dependent poor farm and policed reservation its people, at least most of them, must be employable, and not as charity cases.

Planning has been called the systematic management of assets. One is unlikely to continue to have assets unless one is constantly concerned with the rates of return on one's product line. The city's services are its product line. For too long their comparative contribution to the earning power of the city has remained unevaluated. Once the city is seen as a business, the business of the people who inhabit it, the appraisal of the city's services in terms of their usefulness to maintain and increase the city's earnings, of what the city's people can earn, seems the best of good sense. At present the city is seen largely as an affair of consumption. It has expenses and taxes, but properly speaking these are not seen as investments in the income-generating power of a local economy. While we think of the city as under some constraint to balance its fiscal books, we only rarely think of its necessity to balance its economic books, to maintain a viable local economy. When we do recognize that the central city has an unviable economy we expect its deficits to be made up from without.

A permanently nonviable local economy can only continue because the outside society is paying it as an institution to store people much as we store grain. Though this kind of special role is possible for the city and its bureaucracies, as a social system it is as destructive as the Indian reservation. To avoid this state the older city needs to pursue a vigorous policy to restore the viability of its local

economy and, in so doing, its relation with the outside society from one of dependence to the equal exchange of
trading partners both of whom have something of value to
offer.

As a beginning the city needs a systematic inventory of
its assets and its liabilities. A start can be made by inventorying the employed and employable population. But
these, of course, are not the only sources of revenue to the
city. Frequently, the city's most highly paid and productively employed people do not live in the city. Whether
the jobs that they hold, or the existing proportion of the
jobs they hold, is necessary and desirable needs looking
into. But the nonresident employees apart, the city badly
needs to know what skills its people have, how they are
presently employed, underemployed, and unemployed. The
state of its inhabitants' employment is the single most important fact about the city. The improvement of that state
is the city's single most important task which, if undertaken effectively, is the most powerful way for the city to
earn the loyalty and commitment of its people. To provide
jobs for the deserving, frequently in private as well as public employment, is an old city tradition. If the city and its
politics were to move from patronage and special privilege
to something close to a modern and efficient employment
service that could and would place its inhabitants in jobs
—and better jobs—this would be a new and healthy development.

It seems scarcely credible that, after all the funds that
have been spent on planning, the city should still lack an
inventory of its human resources. Such, however, is the
case. The city knows far more about the condition of its
physical structures than it does about the capabilities, or
for that matter the health, of its people. We have property
inventories but not people inventories. Our national system
of accounting, the census, can only with the greatest diffi-

culty be made to yield data of any value for human-resource planning and utilization. The city will have to do its own job of inventorying not only the skills its people possess but their aptitudes and capacity to receive training.

At present, ignorance of the characteristics of the city's manpower pool is compounded by our lack of reliable information about the real requirements of jobs in the present job mix of industry, not to speak of likely future changes in the composition of the job mix. Ivar Berg's studies showing the dependence of industry personnel departments on a set of academic credentials that seem poorly related, if at all, either to job requirements or to job performance highlight a major difficulty. The city and its people do not know what industry really needs since personnel people have hidden behind academic credentials instead of determining the actual testable requirements for job performance and, where relevant, promotability. The federal government has not been much help either, though some of the experiences of the armed forces should suggest to the city that many of its people can be trained to perform well in jobs of complexity and responsibility.

Our lack of realistic knowledge of industry's job requirements seriously impedes any efforts to improve the relevance of the city's educational investment to the employability of the students who are its product. In dollars, the expenditure on education is a major feature of the city's budget. Given its straitened fiscal condition, the city can no longer afford to have an expenditure of this magnitude fail to pay for itself in the contribution it makes to the earning power of the city's population. Such a view might seem philistine. But in its defense one might cite Aristotle, who said one must first be able to live before being able to live well. By getting the schools to consciously use their very real potential in order to facilitate the employability of its youth the city would give urban education a goal it sorely needs. As it is, the college gatekeepers and the ultimate validation of Ivy League acceptability are of doubtful use for the guidance of even affluent suburban schools. For the schools of the city they are an unmitigated disaster, a status symbol that has little magic and heavy cost.

True, powerful political pressure will be needed to restructure the thrust of the city's educational structure. It is locked into a well-worn set of ruts. To seek change courts not only the bitter opposition of vested educational interests but arouses public and minority fears that what is proposed is a second-class education for their children. And it is true that education has for so long been modeled as an upper-class status symbol and luxury that bringing it in vital contact with the world of work does seem to vulgarize it. Since the Greeks the aristocratic disdain for the useful has been the hallmark of liberal education. The city and its people can no longer afford such an education.

But though the city needs to assure itself that the education its schools provide promotes their students' employability, it cannot abandon all concern with holding and even attracting middle-class people. To do so it will have to offer schools and schooling of college preparatory quality that make it possible for middle-class parents and others seeking college for their children to live in the city without feeling that by doing so they must sacrifice their children or undergo the expense of private education. Without such schooling the city will lose not only middle-class business and professional families, but its teachers and police as well.

Thus the challenge for the city and those who run its schools is to develop an education that prepares both for early entry into the world of work and adult roles and for college and professional schools. Both educational objectives should be furthered by a school system that seeks to pay its way and encourages its students to pay their way by participating in the adult life of the city. Recently schoolmen have rediscovered the importance of the world of work and of student participation in adult roles for the motivation and sense of subject relevance they can produce. Work-study is already, in a small way, being made to build bridges between the isolated world of education and the economy it should at once serve, evaluate, and ultimately assist in advancing. By making the school seriously serve the serious purposes of its students and the society in which it lives such programs will help it regain the authority of competence and relevance, much as with athletes who feel their coach has something to teach them and they have something to learn about a game they want to play and win. With this regained there is every hope that the disorder of the schools, reflecting the disorder of the society, may give way to the discipline and authority of credible competence in the attainment of shared purposes.

But even with the best of good will and the most competent of direction the school system will find it difficult to function if 20 to 40 per cent of the youth it turns out are unemployed. If unemployment and dirty, dead-end, low-pay, and casual jobs are all that most such youth can expect on graduation, the school can hardly become a credible enterprise.

The most useful thing for youth and the city is an honest effort to face up realistically to the situation. If, as the society presently functions, education does not pay off, is it a waste of scarce resources that could be better used some other way? If the name of the game is to get these youths decently employed, how much of our educational effort is relevant to such an objective? Just how serious for the city is the heavy unemployment and underemployment of its young people? These questions need to be asked. When they are, it may well appear that by no means all that the city could do, even with its limited resources, is being done.

If the unemployment and underemployment of young black males is critical for both crime in the streets and the demoralization of the school system, this is a far from trivial statistic. It may be one of the more important causes of wholesale losses in property values, the rise in dependency and illegitimacy, and the waste of massive expenditures in education that are, under the circumstances, foredoomed to failure. But the way the society presently keeps books, the unemployment of these young blacks is a small matter. We are simply not set to respond to it. What we are prepared to do is spend millions on police and police hardware to make streets safe through a program that all our best staff work tells us is bound to fail. Of course, the people who run the city know better, but that is what emerges from Washington. And the city, like some overgrown Springdale, tags along where the money is. Were it an enlightened cooperative that kept business-like books, it would be well aware of the real costs of this youth unemployment and underemployment and would try its level best to find out what could be done to alter the situation.

The police, for example, could do far more to promote safe streets if, instead of the futile attempt to process these juveniles through a hopelessly inefficient criminal justice system, they used their special knowledge of the population at hazard to create an effective early-warning system. If only there were a way to pay police for preventing crime rather than arresting criminals a different scoring system with less entertainment value but more causal efficacy might develop. Skolnik's *Justice Without Trial* is a revealing look at how all the players in the criminal justice game as it is currently played do what will make them look good, even though the outcome, public entertainment apart, is calamitous. Present procedures, as Norval Morris points out, are hopelessly ineffective. If only some 2 per cent of crimes led to their perpetrators being caught, tried, convicted, and sent to jail and if, as Ramsay Clark maintains, some 80 per cent of those going to jail return to crime,[2] there has to be a better way. One better way might be to use police knowledge of who are criminals or likely to become criminals, not to try to catch them and send them to reform schools that do not reform but to put them in touch with those who could at least attempt to interest them in alternatives to criminal occupations.

Then there is the problem of the city's aged, who account for a quarter of the total population. For the most part they have failed to earn enough to make adequate provision for themselves. Neither social security, savings, pensions, nor their families are sufficient for them to live in decency. Most approaches to their problems consider what they ideally should have and proceed to lament the present lack of funds and await a better day or lobby for its coming. It seems reasonable to believe that for some time and for most, to be old and live in the city will be to be poor.

The city, itself in straitened circumstances, can best help those in the same fix by helping them to help themselves. First and foremost it can help provide the aged who are able to work with opportunities to supplement such incomes as they presently have. Even small additional sums can make major differences and, apart from the income, the occupation and sense of continuing usefulness is an incalculable gain. In addition to assisting the aged to obtain employment, the city can assist the aged to use their resources more efficiently. By planning to achieve adequate densities of the old-age population, for example, it should be possible to make health and other services available, reduce transport costs, and create economies of scale.

The aged, moreover, are an important factor in the decline of the city's housing stock. While their incomes are sharply declining, they are pressed by both the burden of property taxes and the rising costs of maintaining the older structures they inhabit. Though sentimentally attached to their housing and neighborhoods, the housing they live in is often highly inappropriate for their needs, being both too large and too costly for them to maintain adequately. Yet where this housing is single family, it is often suitable, with appropriate repair, for occupancy by families with children. The resulting mismatch in the use of the city's housing stock is productive of blight and premature obsolescence. Clearly then it is in the interest of the city and the aged alike to provide them with alternative housing accommodations more suitable to their needs and more within their means and the means it is within the city's power to provide them.

In general the city needs a comprehensive approach to managing its housing stock. Given the present tendency of the older city to lose far more of its housing through deterioration, blight, and abandonment than it acquires through new construction, an approach that takes a systemic view of the factors producing the current trend is in order. That is the point Loewenstein and Hermann make in their *San Francisco Community Renewal Program: A Summary:*

The need for a city wide approach to urban renewal activity has become obvious as more and more communities, including San Francisco, have shown the project-by-project approach to be incapable of dealing with the huge renewal task facing them. Such an approach was not even eliminating blighted areas at the same rate at which blight was occurring in other parts of the city.[3]

Bailing a leaky boat, however profitable to those involved in the bailing, makes little sense except to gain time in which to repair and stop the leaks.

Basic to the city's housing dilemma are the relations between the incomes of its inhabitants and housing costs—maintenance, taxes, insurance, and financing—which often leave the others with too small a margin to encourage any other policy than milking and disinvestment. When we add problems of crime, vandalism, trash, poor services, and so on, disinvestment becomes the norm and the fly-by-night profit-skimming in-and-out operator takes over.

In dealing with its housing problems the city has been bemused by a moralizing rhetoric that, with a specious benevolence toward the poor, has somehow assumed and caused others to assume that the poverty of the housing was owing not to their poverty but to the villainy of convenient devils called "slumlords." This has led to attempts to solve the problem through denunciation and magic. But as Cloward and Piven have pointed out,[4] when the city of New York under so impeccable a liberal as Mayor Lindsay took over property from the slumlords, its practice was no different and for the same economic reasons. Anthony Downs has pointed out that our food marketbasket standard of poverty yields a vastly lower figure than would be obtained by costing out what is officially regarded as the minimum standards of housing decency and building the poverty line on this base rather than on just food.[5] It is not done because such a poverty line figure would be out of sight. Ignoring it, however, does not make it go away. If minimally decent housing for a family of four requires an annual income of more than $7,500 while we are using a food basket poverty line of $3,500, then we are merely deceiving ourselves about the extent of the poverty problem. Such self-deception, which it is in the misconceived interest of a curious combination of liberals, construction trades, realtors, financial institutions, and material suppliers to continue, prevents a realistic approach to the housing problem. When very large numbers of people cannot afford decent housing, only three real alternatives exist: increase people's incomes, decrease housing costs, and/or review the standards of housing decency.

The city can, to a degree, and must move on all three of these fronts. Using the city's various capabilities to increase people's incomes is perhaps for the long pull the most important and most neglected strategy. The rigidities and malfunctioning of the city and metropolitan labor market are an important causal factor in the failure of these markets to perform as economists say they should in mobilizing and matching both the demand for and the supply of the varied labor resources in the area. Though education is perhaps the city's greatest tool for raising its people's incomes (as it is its greatest dollar investment), a city employment service to program and galvanize federal, state, and private agencies as well as acting on its own would also make a major contribution. The city also needs a realistic plan to deal with the actual transportation of its labor force, both resident and nonresident. The powerful thrust of interests that benefit from the construction of costly public monuments and the liberal and ecological alliance threaten massive and ill-considered investments in mass transit that may have little payoff in ridership or environmental improvement. Such investments can gobble up capital that is badly needed for other more productive investments and saddle the city, as has the transit authority, with expensive maintenance and carrying charges, aggressive, costly union demands, and a system that does little to solve the people's real transport needs.

In addition to seeking to increase its people's income the city can attempt to reduce their housing burden by using its own capacity and that of the federal and state governments to reduce financing costs. Through aggressive use of federal tools Cincinnati, for example, is achieving a major advance in the rehabilitation of much of its older housing stock. What the city needs for the flexible management of its housing stock is a redevelopment corporation that can both purchase and condemn property and make a wide range of loans to homeowners and developers.

But with all the efforts the city or anyone else, federal or state, is likely to be able to make, the gap between people's incomes and the costs of official minimally decent housing standards will remain large. This inevitably raises the question of the validity of the applicable standards. Codes, both with respect to new construction and, for the older city, housing maintenance, need careful examination; in all likelihood they are counterproductive in securing adequate new housing or fostering adequate practical maintenance. The utilization of other than high-priced union labor or of mixes of union and nonunion—particularly owners, tenants, and youth in work-study programs— needs exploration. Much of the time of poorer people is a free good. If, without undue costs of supervision and material wastage, it could be put to use maintaining old housing or even building new housing, both the city's and their real income would increase. Having done this sort of thing in the Philippines and elsewhere under the name of community development, we can ill afford not to practice it at home.

It is in the interest of the city and most, though not all, of its people that its manpower resource and its physical capital be put to their best use. For this to happen some people must be able to combine the labor, materials, and stock of physical capital in such a way as to produce a profit. Demagogy and a misdirected and counterproductive concern for the poor has caused profit to become a dirty word. But whether we are socialist or capitalist we pay a heavy price if we fail to concern ourselves with the efficient allocation of resources. Profitability is not under all circumstances the best and only criterion for the efficient allocation of resources. It is, however, a criterion that we and the city neglect at our peril. And unfortunately for the city, it is a method of accounting that is rarely practiced in its own resource allocation. This failure is a major reason why cities are in financial straits and why urban economies stagger under unproductive burdens that erode their viability. A cooperative, even a humane one, must be able to balance its books or fail; so, too, must the city.

Hong Kong seems to achieve effortlessly the transformation of refugee Chinese peasants with minor amounts of capital into a functioning part of an economic system that earns its own way. In all likelihood the culture of unremitting toil to which the peasants are inured, the lash of hunger, and the superiority of their life chances, such as they are, accounts for some of this success in Hong Kong. But there is another factor of undetermined but possibly immense importance—the ready availability of entrepreneurial talent to shape up this labor force and produce and merchandise a product. Entrepreneurship as a scarce factor is well recognized throughout the Far East. But in this country, the city's educational system, and certainly the universities, have shown little talent for developing a supply of small-businessmen. Business schools are far more adept at turning out bureaucrats for I.B.M. and General Electric than entrepreneurs capable of shaping up a black labor force and developing and merchandizing products. The blacks that business schools train seldom return to the ghetto; usually they are slotted into a showcase career in the larger corporations. Black businessmen themselves are so obsessed, perhaps rightly, with the competition and the meagerness of the rewards that they show little real interest in expanding their number through developing new talent. And the activities of white industry are more for publicity than profit.

There may be no recipe for turning out small-businessmen in the quantity and quality that the city

needs, but it surely is worth investing major efforts to discover whether this talent can be developed in, or at least
lured to, the city. Raymond Vernon and others see the
older city as having continuing use as a seed bed for new
industry and as a place still rich in external economies for
those small concerns with unstandardized inputs and outputs. Such expressions of confidence stem from the famil-
iarity of Harvard scholars with New York's garment and
high-style clothing industry; they need to be given more
flesh and blood through identifying similar patterns and
logics in other industries from whose study the city could
profit. If the city cannot rely on a ready supply of small-
businessmen to do its economic thinking for it, it may itself have to undertake the research and development
needed to demonstrate profit opportunities in possible
combinations of its manpower and physical capital.

City planning has been so immersed in the beaux arts
tradition, so bound up in brick and mortar, that it has only
recently begun to concern itself with the economics of the
city. The federal government and its urban renewal requirements have done little to focus concern on the over-
all problems of the city's economy. And the model-city
program has done little beyond focusing the attention of
city planning on more extended project areas and thus
bringing it into what may become a fruitful dialogue with
the residents of the planned-for area. The fault of this
scarcely lies with city planning alone. Academic economics
has but just discovered the city. The first text on urban
economics is only a few years old, and economic base studies are not much older. As John Dyckman has remarked,[6]
our knowledge, or lack of knowledge, of the city's economy
derives from a national breakdown of income shares. In
other words, our national accounts tell us little about what
makes cities tick, tick differently, and tick better than one
another.

Still and all, the city could turn its planning agency into a research and development capability to study the profit opportunities that may be latent in the city. Such an agency could gather relevant data on the experience of other cities. Above all, it could model a variety of enterprises to see how the city and its policies, tax and other, were affecting their potential for success and what alteration in policies might improve their viability in the city. Such an examination would need to be brutal and frank and would take all the political guts and support the city as a cooperative for its inhabitants could muster. In a city such as Newark, with an 8 per cent plus tax rate on full valuation, wide-scale property abandonment, and a monumental disinterest on the part of investors, it might be necessary to bite the bullet and decide on service retrenchment instead of waiting for a state or federal bailout. Indeed, a careful examination of the cost effectiveness of the various services might well reveal that in terms of really significant contribution to the inhabitants' well-being, it was possible to make far less money go a far longer way. Here accountability contracts offer a major avenue for exploring the possibility of accomplishing the really important objectives of such services in far more cost-effective ways. In this way the older city could join the Los Angeles upper-class cooperative of the Lakewood Plan in the use of purchasing-agent techniques that Robert Bish has found promising. Any attempt to do this, of course, must run the gauntlet of opposition from public-employee unions, their allies, state requirements legislating the status quo and the folk conservatism of the voters, and the identification of many of them with the public employees.

Ultimately the city needs to face up to a choice: Does it want policies that put tax and other burdens on industry and housing resulting in economic stagnation and blight and abandonment of its housing or policies that create the incentives to maintain and expand industry, employment, and its housing stock? Some of the existing public services are vital to the city's economy, to the health and employment of its people. The city badly needs to know what these are. Given the functioning of cities abroad and of American cities in the past, and some even now, it seems highly doubtful that the levels and costs of many American cities' municipal services are essential to their continued well-being. There is even credible expert testimony to the possibility that, without counterproductive restrictions, an essentially better job with fewer personnel at less total expense could be achieved. Given the fiscal constraints of many American cities, the possibility that this is the case needs to be diligently explored and accurately determined. What needs doing may be politically difficult and painful, but we badly need to know whether doing it would make a major difference in these dimensions. If modeling the facts of both industry and housing shows that it would, it should then be possible to work out with employees and the states the transition that would free the cities to help themselves. America's cities need not follow the same course as America's railways.

Sol Linowitz, chairman of the Urban Coalition, has called on industry to make it possible for their employees to follow them to the suburbs when they relocate from the city. The figures he cites for the proportion of new jobs requiring unskilled or low-skilled labor that are developing in the suburbs justify his fear that many in the city will be deprived of the chance to be employed in those jobs for which they are presently most fit. Paul Davidoff and other planners and public-interest lawyers are trying hard to open up the suburbs and get action on low-income housing for low-income and minority residents. The Advisory Committee on Intergovernmental Relations has had at least one task committee urge a positive approach to the problem, and Governor Romney seems still strong in his advocacy of opportunity for the poor in suburbia. But, the administration's over-all position is at best ambiguous and much of the President's and the attorney-general's positions seem hostile. However, Edward Banfield and his colleagues on the President's Task Force on Model Cities say,

Any solution to the fundamental problem of the large cities will have to be found largely in the suburban fringes, the area where most of the growth is taking place. The key measures will be ones that hasten the movement of the poor and the black out of the inner-city slums and semislums and to the places where job and other opportunities are relatively good: we have in mind particularly measures to maintain an active demand for low skilled workers, to raise incomes (as, for example, the Administration's family assistance program would do) to improve job training, to eliminate barriers that prevent the poor and the black from securing housing in fringe areas (unreasonable zoning ordinances and building codes, for example) and to repeal laws the tendency of which is to price the low skilled worker out of the labor market altogether.[7]

This view sees the major solution to the city's problem in the transfer of its poor to the suburban fringe where the growing edge of low-skilled jobs is now preponderantly located.

Yet the possibility of achieving such a transfer in the near future appears dim. Even if all restrictions were dropped on the entrance of low-income people, black and white, to the suburbs it would be a long time before any significant migration could take place. The bulk of the housing that low-income people can afford is in the city and the older suburbs. The report of the Douglas Commission gives scant hope that we will see any dramatic reductions in construction costs in the near future and the same is true of interest and land costs.

For a long time, therefore, the bulk of the nation's low-income population will continue to inhabit the central city and its older suburbs. If they are to avail themselves of the growing edge of low-skilled and unskilled jobs in the suburban fringe we will need a land-use and a transportation strategy that will make these jobs available to them. If suburban land use could be more effectively controlled so as to mass the location of industry in a few large industrial parks, a mass transit system of express busses might help bridge the gap between where our biggest stock of low-rent housing is and where the growing edge of low-skill jobs are. The city could even have a part in bringing this about. Many of the suburban towns and municipalities have open acreage but lack the financial and engineering resources of the city to develop it. It should be possible, where state law permits, for the city to enter into partnership with some of its suburbs to develop their open land for industry and participate in the income and employment opportunities such a development could generate. It is even possible that, working with the city, the suburbs might be prepared to open up a certain amount of their land to low-income housing for residents of the city who were going to work in the jointly sponsored industrial parks.

But, realistically, it is hard to believe that the suburbs are rapidly going to open themselves up to low-income housing to any extent, except as in the past through blight, decay, and takeover. In any event, the great bulk of low-rent housing will remain where it presently is. Nor is it likely that tax-hungry suburbs will, without far more state compulsion than seems likely, agree on land-use controls that will so locate new industrial growth as to facilitate access to it by mass transportation from the city.

Under the circumstances it is a source of wonder that industry can locate so inappropriately with respect to the source of its labor supply. Either the industrialists who have made the location decisions are fools, which is possible, or as is more likely they do not want the labor force of which Linowitz speaks and are suburbanizing in part as a means of escaping having to use it. If this is indeed an important part of the motivation, and there is reason to think it is, there is not only a suburban property-owner interest in blocking the access of low-income and minority peoples to the fringe but an industry interest as well. If such is the case, it will be a long time before such powerful opposition can be overcome.

It will be unfortunate for the city if its future depends on any rapid, sizable departure of its present low-income population. This just is not likely to happen. Is it too much to hope that a good deal of the problem could be overcome by the development of this low-income, low-skill population to the point where it could satisfactorily fill more of the higher-skill jobs now in the city as well as other jobs that could be developed there? It has been stated that the imbalance is not so much between the size of the city's present population and the number of jobs remaining in the city as between the skill requirements of these jobs and the educational level of the city's present population. Ivar Berg has called in serious question the validity of the educational credentials used as surrogates for any adequate testing of actual aptitudes for job performance. Yet before the city gives up on the ability of its present population, or at least a significant part of it, to meet the real requirements of the jobs now existing in the city, it will want to explore very carefully both the possibilities of raising the performance capacity of its population to meet realistic job needs and of restructuring existing jobs so as to make them performable within the training range of the present population. The experience of both the armed forces and some of the major hospitals gives some ground for hoping this may be to a considerable extent possible.

As Christopher Jencks has pointed out and as the experience of the hospitals bears witness, a major problem is not so much imparting appropriate skills as providing adequate work motivation and discipline. This is a problem that will have to be solved if the city is to remain tenable for those businesses that now remain. To expect any considerable number of highly skilled businesses with that kind of personnel to persist in the midst of a sullen, un- and underemployed ghetto that knows these jobs are for a race apart is the height of folly. The businesses will only begin to be safe when enough of the poor have a visible stake in their protection. As for the city, it has little alternative but to seek to give what is rapidly becoming the major part of its population a stake in its industry. Lacking such a stake the results are predictable, and all efforts at policing are likely to prove ineffective. Indeed, if the city seeks to hold and increase its middle and stable working class as residents, it must make a major effort to lock the lower class in occupations and roles that will involve it in the maintenance of an effective normative order.

Professor Burch of the Harvard Business School maintains that the older city must find new uses for its plant and people since it can no longer contain within its jurisdiction the full range of occupations and strata that have now spread throughout the metropolitan area. A major role for the city is in the growing sector of the services, especially the health industry. Next to tourism, health is probably the most important growth industry in the country. Unlike tourism, it is backed up by a heavy unmet and effective demand whose inflationary pressure will be a long time in diminishing. Health is a labor-intensive field, making use of much of the low- and unskilled labor that Linowitz and the President's Task Force on Model Cities see as having to suburbanize to find employment. Though unskilled health jobs have been menial and unrewarding, this condition seems on the point of change. The ditchdiggers of the health industry are on the threshold of mechanization as were their predecessors in construction. Recent experience in the hospitals shows that job development and the creation of career ladders to overcome the barriers of licensure are possible. Despite disciplinary difficulties and fits of delusions of grandeur, the experience of the hospitals pioneering the new employment frontier indicates that the lower-class employees can be trained for technical, skilled jobs and succeed in career occupations.

The Japanese on the West Coast, despite assiduous pursuit of education, were consigned to jobs as yard boys, servants, and market gardeners until after World War II when the Oriental broke through into the professions and attained a higher position in the job hierarchy than the whites. Of course, the family and culture of the Orientals differentiate their position from that of the American Negro. Despite such differences, it is altogether possible that the health industry with its enormous potential for expansion may provide the means for a massive breakthrough of blacks into professional careers—and with it their own self-respect and the society's as well. The black doctor and medical technician may be to the blacks what the Japanese physicist, mathematician, and architect have been to the Oriental victims of race prejudice and job discrimination. For the city such a development would be of the utmost importance in transforming a human liability that is draining the city's resources through unemployment, underemployment, dependency, and crime into a productive human asset making a major contribution to its own and the city's growth. Success in the health industry, moreover, would serve as an example that could lead to success in other areas.

The health industry also offers a major opportunity to utilize the city's unused and underutilized plant. Nursing homes, geriatric care, child care—all the health services that require nursing and some medical supervision can, in principle, make use of the city's stock of apartments and large older buildings. If the city would both promote the development and stringently supervise the quality of the services, it could command a growing, better met market for this kind of health care. As a health center with a rounded complement of capabilities, from multiphasic automated health-testing to produce economies of scale with medical parks and residence neighborhoods for doctors, nurses, technicians and other employees to research and development efforts mounted by universities, hospitals, and industry to produce new bioelectronic and other technology, the city has a major interest in pushing health and the health industry as a major use of its people, plant, and location. By pioneering low-cost health delivery to the poor, as Columbia's School of Physicians and Surgeons in New York, the city would not only reduce waste in its own health delivery system but produce major payoffs in methods and techniques for the improvement of the health-care system as a whole.

There is a general belief that all but a few—the wealthy, childless couples—have lost interest in the city. The middle class and even the stable working class are thought to be overwhelmingly committed to life in suburbia, with the older city no more than a central business district, an occasional place to shop, and the location of sports arenas, theaters, symphonies, and other cultural attractions. This may be true for many, but it may by no means be true for all or anywhere near all. The change in life style of the contemporary youth culture should make the homogenized uniformity of the suburban enclave a drag. The young medical students who want to practice community medicine, unlike their professors, will hopefully want to live in the city with their patients. The public-interest lawyers may well wish to do the same. A vigorous and growing breed of craftsmen who work with their hands and brains to create artistic objects that are now in demand in our affluent society even among the lower-middle and the working class, need cheap housing, cheap shops, and a market for their wares. They are quite capable of putting sweat equity and technical competence into the restoration of property that offers at a low price a shop and a roof over their heads.

The steeply ascending costs of construction, suburban land, and money make the "new car market" of suburban housing by no means so clearly a better bargain than the "old car market" of the city. Suburban land prices are already turning more and more new construction toward apartment buildings. Even the family that wants to own its own home may find that its best chance to do so at a price it can afford is in the city and the older suburb.

The city's major problems in taking advantage of its improved competitive position in the housing market are security, education, and taxes. Most middle-class people, on being asked why they do not avail themselves of the city's better housing buys, usually respond, "We don't feel safe on the streets of the city, and we don't feel that our children are safe in the city's schools. Further, we don't feel that the city's schools give a quality education, by which we usually mean one where the youth culture and the teachers are oriented toward college preparation and entrance." Take all these things together (plus higher taxes), and the city lacks pulling power, even for those who appreciate its housing and the other amenities that go with city living.

So many regard the city as hopeless because of its lack of revenues that the conditions of poor security, poor schools, poor other services, and high taxes are taken as unavoidable. The only means for their remedy is thought to be an increase in funds, and the only practical way to

182

achieve this is thought to be revenue-sharing. This definition of the city's situation turns its leadership's attention
away from any serious thought of what the city can do to
help itself. It is the politics of purchased solutions, which
assumes the existence of some well-stocked store with public goods from whose shelves, if it only had the money, the
city could buy what it requires. Yet our foreign-aid experience should by this time have taught us that you can not
buy any honey with money and that only those who are
prepared to help themselves can be helped.

Those, especially on the left, who see the existing city as
a husk empty of nutrients because of its fiscal crisis, accept
the definition of the city as powerless and hence as largely
valueless. They see the blacks finally coming to power in
the city after it has been drained dry and left a crumbling
mass of structures encumbered with a still largely white
public bureaucracy allied with the construction unions in
the continued exploitation of what remains of the city.
There is a measure of truth to this view as Newark and
other cities attest. But this is by no means the whole story,
it is only true to the extent that the city cannot be used
now as it once was as a cooperative device for its inhabitants to pool their resources and meet their needs.

The paradigm case of the value of institutionalized cooperation for the poorest of the poor is the Black Muslim
Church, whose capacity to turn criminals, drug addicts,
prostitutes, dependents, and other unpromising material
into people with self-respect who evince capacity for self-
help is a major example of behavioral modification in action without benefit of Skinner. Its ability to dramatically
change its members' real standard of living by increasing the effectiveness of their resource utilization is of espe-
cial interest to those who, like the city, believe that all improvements must be paid for with cash. The difference
between the scene depicted in Lyford's *Airtight Cage* and

the neighborhood of a Black Muslim Church illustrates the extent to which self-help, even with no significant infusion of outside cash, can make a favorable difference. The virtues of the Muslims may seem bourgeois and despite a lurid language of nationalism and white diabolism, they are. So, in fact, are the virtues preached by Mao and Castro. They appeal to most who wish seriously to build, whether they are socialist or capitalist. What the Black Muslim Church shows is that the effectiveness with which people utilize the resources they have can count as much and more than their absolute amount.

The Black Muslim Church is useful as an example of how people in the worst of conditions, with meager resources, without outside aid and frequently in the face of great outside hostility, can dramatically improve their condition. This, of course, does no more than refute any universal denial of the power of self-help through organized cooperation. We have always known that some churches, by intensely involving their members, could sustain them in adversity and convert their individually weak resources into considerable collective strength.

Such indeed was at one time the function of the older city. The city-state was itself a church in Greece, although its later embodiments were far from secular. But the open city of the nation-state of market capitalism has free-floating producers and consumers rather than citizens. Unlike a Black Muslim Church it is a secular institution, tolerant of a diverse citizenry and of a noncitizenry that uses its site without according it any allegiance whatever. In Robert Nisbet's sense it has lost function and hence community. Increasingly the city of the poor and the disadvantaged, the aged, the discriminated against, and the deviant, the city needs to recover function if it is to survive as a viable economy and a viable normative order. In doing so it will find its best chance to regain community and so re-create a citizenry with shared purposes who can sustain a legitimate leadership and an accepted and acceptable normative order.

If the city is to become a humane cooperative devoted to the improvement of the social and economic well-being of its inhabitants, who will take the lead in such an enterprise? Who is really interested in building the cities as men elsewhere interest themselves in building nations? Who see in the cities more than sentimental relics of a glorious past without future or function, the obsolescing abode of the poor, the deviant and declining industry? The rhetoric of restoring the cities abounds. There is scarcely a political figure, business leader, union leader, television commentator, or pundit who does not have a nostrum for the cities' rebirth. Yet who in the city can and will lead it in the arduous and difficult task of city building?

The business community has already largely suburbanized its residence and is increasingly suburbanizing its investment. Its concern with the city is largely one of do-good projects that reap their reward in favorable publicity and a good corporate image. Yet its most important contribution could be doing what it is best at, finding a way of putting men and materials to work so as to make a profit. Unfortunately the normal present course is for businesses, like real estate and others, to make their money from milking property and disinvesting. Even worse, many businesses, engineering firms, architects, construction companies, and so on make money by inducting the hard-pressed city to invest in circuses, monuments, and well-publicized patent solutions such as mass transit.

Neither business nor the press really concerns itself with the need for competent research into ways and means of meeting the city's problems. A penchant for action results in both press and business advocating major public investments without any comprehension of their cost effectiveness. These are like so much patent medicine—what everybody knows is the currently fashionable remedy for what ails the cities. Others, the engineering firms, the contractors, the unions, the public relations firms, and all who make this a business have a more obvious stake in the promotion of projects from which, however worthless to the city, they stand to profit. It is not surprising that the city, like the Pentagon, has its own military industrial complex. Too bad for the city that it lacks the Pentagon's purse.

The white middle class and the ethnic working class in the city seem no longer to have any confidence that they can fight more than a delaying action. The middle class takes its lead from business with which it frequently has a love-hate relationship depending on whether those involved are liberal professionals, conservatives, small shopkeepers, or white-collar employees. The ethnics take their lead from the unions and the church. The lead of the most powerful city-based unions, the construction trades, is both conservative and basically unconcerned with more than job protectionism. The mass production unions, the auto workers, the petroleum workers, the teamsters, and the retail clerks have constituencies that increasingly divide between city and suburb. Though these unions at least have blacks in their membership, the more liberal and consumer-oriented position of the leadership is held in check by the conservatism of the rank and file and the necessary concern with the politics of organization maintenance. Beyond this the unions feel they must respect the public-employee unions who stand in the same relation to the city as do they to their employers. Though the position is ambiguous—the private-sector union members are citizens needing services, and these unions have on occasion, particularly the teamsters, concerned themselves with city services—for the most part their basic concern is wages and working conditions on the job, not consumption. They tend therefore to ally themselves with, rather than fight against, the public-employee unions.

Since they are poor and disadvantaged, in need of the positive things the city could do and hurt by the harmful things that it does do, the blacks objectively have the greatest reason for wishing to see the city turned into a humane cooperative for the improvement of their lot. However, if this be their objective interest it has not penetrated their subjective consciousness. Victims of a history in which whatever indigenous political culture they brought to America was destroyed, they have little capacity to develop a legitimate political leadership. Lower-class black culture, according to Kenneth B. Clark, author of *Dark Ghetto*,[8] lacks all respect for the black middle class and recognizes no legitimate leadership roles. Without legitimate leadership roles it is impossible to create an effective authority structure to mobilize human and material resources. James Wilson has commented on the inability of the blacks of Chicago, though numbering a million, to collect more than a few thousands of dollars for the only private hospital open to blacks in the city. The endemic hustle and the corrosive distrust of people for leaders and leaders for one another debilitates the potential political force that blacks could exercise. Despite the romanticization of the juvenile gangs and self-deceptive slogans of brother and community, the painful fact remains, as with the Blackstone Rangers, that black is more apt to exploit black than join with him to improve the common condition.

The most important, the best organized, the most concerned, and the most destructive of the city are the public employees and their unions. With no intention to bankrupt the city they lack any structured incentive to do otherwise. The low productivity of the service industry would by itself ensure that in their simple effort to keep pace with

comparable wages in the private sector the employee
unions would face the city with staggering, mounting costs.
But in addition, there is no incentive to reward efficiency:
Manpower is used instead of technological advance to improve working conditions, and such technology as already
exists is ignored or, when used, rendered ineffective. This
is bad enough, but there is little reason to doubt that much
of the city's expenditures in education, health, and police,
to name three of the largest city services, are not only unproductive but counterproductive.

One might consider the outlook for the city as grim and
well-nigh hopeless. What could lead one to believe that a
business such as a city with so feckless a management,
such small incentive to make painful, difficult changes,
such powerful public-employee unions, an apathetic public, divided blacks, a barely involved business community,
a middle class that has flight as an option, and a media
whose role is critic can be restored to solvency? The
hope of the city is much the same as the hope of the hospital: Both badly need to orient themselves effectively and
honestly toward those they claim to serve. Both need to
cope with hardened bureaucracies entrenched behind licensure and civil service. Both need to face up to the economic facts of life. Both need to use the unused manpower
of their institutions and in doing so restore authority to the
enterprise. Both could benefit from the support a genuine
increase in effective service might engender. Both are in
danger of letting fiscal matters go from bad to worse. Both
may, and here the hospital is better off than the city, have
new blood among their experts and the upward moving
poor to press for both more effective and more economical
performance. In the young of the schools and the young of
the inner city may be the material to remake institutions.

The older larger city looks much like a railway, and it is
easier to fight for the status quo than to take a present loss

in the hope that the enterprise will eventually be restored. One hopes the city is not all that much like the railways. Its workers have not been fobbed off with false hopes. Unlike the railways, the city could have a management with genuine popular support that unions would have to respect. There is in the trade-union tradition a lingering concern with more than pork-chop unionism. Michael Harrington and others of a socialist persuasion think that from this source some real support for the city as humane cooperative might be evoked. Of all those with power and a rational self-interest in the city's future none have more than the public employees whose own future and that of the city are hopelessly interlocked. Can they be made to see their interest in the city as their cooperative, a producer as well as a consumer cooperative that offers them in every rank a vocation with meaning, challenge, and reward? Can the incentive system of the city unite management, employees, and citizen consumer producers in a humane cooperative to improve the lives of the whole city? These questions will probably remain for the labor movement, the young doctors, the public-interest lawyers, the artists, middle class, and the black leaders, who from widely divergent perspectives see a need for a future in the city.

Notes

1 *The Unwalled City*

1. Max Weber, *The City*, trans. and ed. Don Martindale and Gertrude Neuwirth (New York: The Free Press, paperback ed., 1966), p. 62.

2. George H. Sabine, *A History of Political Theory*, 3rd ed. (New York: Holt, Rinehart & Winston, 1961), chapter 7.

3. Aleksandr I. Solzhenitsyn, *The First Circle* (New York: Harper & Row, 1968).

4. Fustel de Coulanges, *La Cité Antique*, cited in C. H. McIlwain, *The Growth of Political Thought in the West* (New York: Macmillan, 1961), p. 9.

5. Robert Dahl, *Who Governs?: Democracy and Power in an American City* (New Haven: Yale University Press, 1961).

6. Edward Banfield and James Q. Wilson, *City Politics* (Cambridge: Harvard University Press and the M.I.T. Press, 1963).

7. Jay W. Forrester, *Urban Dynamics* (Cambridge: the M.I.T. Press, 1969).

8. Wilbur Thompson, *A Preface to Urban Dynamics* (Baltimore: The Johns Hopkins Press, 1965).

9. David Rosenbaum in *The New York Times*, reprinted by *St. Louis Post-Dispatch*, April 8, 1971.

10. Lyle Fitch, "Alternatives to 'General Revenue Sharing'" (unpublished paper).

11. Sidney P. Marland Jr. in a talk to the Education Writers Association as reported in the *St. Louis Post-Dispatch*, April 18, 1971.

12. James S. Coleman, *Equality of Educational Opportunity*, U.S. Department of H.E.W., Office of Education (Washington, D.C.: U.S. Government Printing Office, 1966).

13. Ivar Berg, *Education and Jobs, The Great Training Robbery* (New York: Praeger, 1970).

14. Abram Flexner, *Universities, American, English, German* (1930; paperback ed., New York: Oxford, 1968).

15. Christopher Jencks, "A Reappraisal of the Most Controversial Educational Document of Our Time," *New York Times Magazine*, August 10, 1969, p. 12ff.

16. Dana L. Spitzer in a series of articles in the *St. Louis Post-Dispatch*.

17. Southwestern Bell, Statement of representative of Southwestern Bell at Conference on Youth Employment, Stouffer's Riverfront Inn, St. Louis, June 1971.

18. Vincent Ostrom, Charles Thiebout, and Robert Warren, "The Organization of Government in Metropolitan Areas: A Theoretical Inquiry," *American Political Science Review* 55 (1961): 831.

19. Kermit Gordon, ed., *Agenda for the Nation* (Washington: Brookings Institution, 1968).

20. Robert Wood, *1400 Governments* (Cambridge: Harvard University Press, 1961).

21. Charles Haar, *The Effectiveness of Metropolitan Planning* (Washington, D.C.: U.S. Government Printing Office, 1964).

22. Robert L. Bish, *The Public Economy of Metropolitan Areas* (Chicago: Markham Publishing Company, 1971).

23. Cf. *The Effectiveness of Metropolitan Planning* (Washington, D.C.: U.S. Government Printing Office, 1964).

2 *Metropolitan Areas: Communities without Governments?*

1. Joseph Lyford, *Airtight Cage* (New York: Harper & Row, 1966).

2. Henry J. Schmandt and Warner Bloomberg, "The Quality of Urban Life," *Urban Affairs Annual Review*, Vol. 3 (1969).

3. Arnold S. Meltsner and Aaron Wildavsy, "Leave City Budgeting Alone! A Survey, Case Study, and Recommendations for Reform in Financing The Metropolis, Public Policy in Urban Economics," ed. John P. Crecine, *Urban Affairs Annual Review*, Vol. 4 (1970).

4. Robert Wood, in various writings.

5. Harold Kaplan, "The Policy-Making Process in Metro Toronto," in Lionel D. Feldman and Michael D. Goldrick, *Politics and Government of Urban Canada* (Toronto: Methuen Publications, 1969), p. 197.

6. W. J. McCordic, "Urban Education: An Experiment in Two-Tiered Administration," in Lionel D. Feldman and Michael D. Goldrick, ed., *Politics and Government of Urban Canada* (Toronto: Methuen Publications, 1969), p. 120.

7. *Ibid.*, p. 119.

8. Gail C. A. Cook, "Public Service Provision in Metropolitan Areas," in Feldman and Goldrick, *Politics and Government of Urban Canada*, p. 86.

9. Alexis de Tocqueville, *Democracy in America*, ed. and abridged by Richard D. Heffner (New York: New American Library, 1956), p. 60.

10. Bernard Frieden, *The Future of Old Neighborhoods* (Cambridge: M.I.T. Press, 1964).

11. Police Colonel Sanders, oral testimony before the National Democratic Platform Committee heard by the author.

12. From the partial text of an address to the New York Rotary Club, "The Contemporary Enlightened Businessman," in *City* (May–June 1971), p. 12.

13. Black Jack is a municipality in St. Louis County that is alleged to have incorporated for the purpose of zoning out a projected low and moderate income housing development. The case is before the courts.

14. Daniel P. Moynihan, *Maximum Feasible Misunderstanding, Community Action in the War on Poverty* (The Free Press, New York, 1969).

15. Feldman and Goldrick, *Politics and Government of Urban Canada*, p. 172.

16. Yoshiko Kasahara, "A Profile of Canada's Metropolitan Centres," in Feldman and Goldrick, *Politics and Government of Urban Canada*, p. 21.

17. *Globe and Daily Mail*, July 16, 1968, p. 5.

18. Hans Blumenfeld, "The Role of the Federal Government in Urban Affairs," in Feldman and Goldrick, *Politics and Government of Urban Canada*, p. 182.

19. Charles L. Schultze, Edward R. Fried, Alice M. Rivlin, and Nancy H. Teeters, *Setting National Priorities: The 1972 Budget*, (Washington, D.C.: The Brookings Institution, 1971).

20. Lyle Fitch, "Alternatives to 'General Revenue Sharing' " (unpublished paper).

3 *The Uneconomic Politics of the City*

1. In various public statements.

2. Frances Fox Piven and Richard Cloward, *Regulating the Poor*, (New York: Pantheon Books, 1971).

3. Anthony Downs, "Moving Toward Realistic Housing Goals," in *Agenda for the Nation*, ed. Kermit Gordon (Brookings Institution: Washington, D.C., 1968).

4. Scott Greer, *Urban Renewal and American Cities* (Indianapolis: Bobbs Merrill, 1965).

5. Bernard J. Frieden, *The Future of Old Neighborhoods* (Cambridge: M.I.T. Press, 1964).

6. Frieden's essay in *Metropolitan Enigma*, ed. James Q. Wilson (Cambridge, Harvard University Press, 1967).

7. Carl Stokes, reported in *Newsweek*, May 5, 1969.

8. Martin Meyerson and Edward Banfield, *Politics, Planning and the Public Interest*, paperback ed. (London: Collier MacMillan, 1964).

Notes

9. James Q. Wilson, "The Mayors versus the Cities," *The Public Interest* (Summer 1969).

10. Wallace Sayre and Herbert Kaufman, *Governing New York City: Politics in the Metropolis* (New York: Russell Sage Foundation, 1960; New York: W. W. Norton, 1965).

11. In Christopher Jencks, "A Reappraisal of the Most Controversial Educational Document of Our Time," *New York Times Magazine*, August 10, 1969, p. 12ff.

12. Michael Harrington, *The Other America—Poverty in The United States* (Macmillan, New York, 1962).

13. John Dyckman and Catherine Wurster, cf. John W. Dyckman, "State Development Planning In A Federal Economic System," Cornell Conference on State Planning, Existing State and Future Trends, Cornell University, Ithaca, March 23, 1966.

14. Raymond Vernon, *Metropolis 1985* (Cambridge: Harvard University Press, 1960).

15. Linowitz in address to the New York Rotary Club cited above, "The Contemporary Enlightened Businessman" in *City* (May–June 1971), p. 12.

16. Dorothy Newman, "The Decentralization of Jobs," *Monthly Labor Review* (May 1967) cited in S. M. Miller and Pamela Roby, *The Future of Inequality* (New York: Basic Books, 1970), p. 117.

17. John Dyckman, in correspondence with author.

18. Chalmers Johnson, *Revolutionary Change* (Boston and Toronto: Little Brown, 1966).

19. S. M. Miller and Pamela Roby, *The Future of Inequality*, pp. 170–174.

20. Edward Banfield, *Unheavenly City: The Nature and the Future of Our Urban Crisis* (Boston: Little Brown & Co., 1968, 1970).

21. Scott Greer, "Put Thy Love in Order," *Social Science Quarterly*, March 1971.

22. Elliot Liebow, *Talley's Corner* (Boston: Little Brown & Co., 1967).

23. Nathan Glazer, "Beyond Income Maintenance—A Note on Welfare in New York City," *Public Interest*, no. 16 (Summer 1969).

24. Paul Lerman, in *Transaction*.

25. *St. Louis Post-Dispatch*, March 12, 1971 reporting Norval Morris' address at a conference on crime, delinquency and the system of justice in Saint Louis.

26. *Ibid.*

27. *Ibid.*

28. Jerome H. Skolnik, *Justice without Trial: Law Enforcement in Democratic Society* (New York: John Wiley & Sons, 1967).

29. Ramsay Clark, *Crime in America, Observations on Its Nature, Causes, Prevention and Control* (New York: Simon & Schuster, 1970).

30. Lyle Fitch, "Alternatives to 'General Revenue Sharing'" (unpublished paper), p. 5ff.

31. David Rosenbaum, in *The New York Times* reprinted by *St. Louis Post-Dispatch*, April 8, 1971.

32. William Baumol, "Macroeconomics of Unbalanced Growth: The Anatomy of Urban Crisis," in *American Economic Review*, June 1967, p. 415.

33. Fitch, "Alternatives to 'General Revenue Sharing'," p. 46.

34. Fitch, *ibid.*

35. David L. Burch, "The Economic Future of City and Suburb," C.E.D. Supplementary Paper No. 30, Committee for Economic Development (New York, 1970).

4 *Local Bourgeois Democracy: Government Without Community?*

1. James Q. Wilson, "Problems in the Study of Urban Politics," A paper prepared for a conference in Commemoration of the 50th anniversary of the Department of Government, Indiana University, Bloomington, November 5–7, 1964, p. 3.

2. Carlo Levi, *Christ Stopped at Eboli*, trans. F. Frenaye (New York: Farrar Straus & Giroux, 1947).

3. James Bryce, *The American Commonwealth* (New York: The Commonwealth Publishing Company, 1908).

4. James Q. Wilson, *Varieties of Police Behavior, The Management of Law and Order in Eight Communities* (Cambridge: Harvard University Press, 1968.)

5. Alan A. Altschuler, *The City Planning Process: A Political Analysis* (Ithaca, N.Y.: Cornell University Press, 1965).

6. Robert H. Salisbury, "Urban Politics, The New Convergence of Power," *Journal of Politics*, 26 (November 1964).

7. Martin Anderson, "The Federal Bulldozer," in *Urban Renewal, The Record and the Controversy*, ed. James Q. Wilson (Cambridge: M.I.T. Press, 1966).

8. William L. Slayton, "Revitalizing the Older City: The Role of Urban Renewal," a paper delivered at the University of Pittsburgh as one of a series sponsored by the Center for Regional Economic Studies, p. 5.

9. Irving Kristol, "Decentralization for What?," *The Public Interest*, no. 11 (Spring 1968).

10. Christopher Jencks, Various pieces in *New Republic* or *Nation*.

11. Willoughby Lathem, M.D., "Technology and Health," *Social Policy*, 1, No. 5 (January–February, 1971), p. 57.

12. Eliot Freidson, "Professionalism: The Doctors' Dilemma," *Social Policy*, 1, No. 5 (January–February 1971), p. 35.

Notes

13. *Ibid*, p. 39.

14. From Dr. Houghton's testimony, published in *Social Policy*, 1, no. 5 (January-February, 1971) p. 17.

15. Vital Statistics, 1969, prepared by Bureau of Statistical Services for the Division of Health, Department of Public Health and Welfare, June 1970, Table 13, pp. 35, 37.

16. U.N.E.S.C.O., Compendium of Social Statistics: 1967, Series K. No. 3 *Infant Mortality Rate*.

17. Arthur J. Vidich and Joseph Bensman, *Small Town in Mass Society* (Princeton, N.J.: Princeton University Press, 1958).

18. Scott Greer and David Minar, "The Political Side of Urban Development and Redevelopment," *Annals of the American Academy of Political and Social Science*, vol. 352 (Philadelphia: March, 1964) p. 67.

19. Sumner M. Rosen, "Upgrading and New Careers in Health," *Social Policy*, 1, no. 5 (January–February 1971), p. 20.

20. The complete telegram was published in *Social Policy*, 1, no. 5 (January–February, 1971), p. 21 ff.

21. Eliot Freidson, "Professionalism: The Doctors' Dilemma," *Social Policy*, 1, no. 5 (January-February 1971) p. 39.

22. Scott Greer and David Minar, "The Political Side of Urban Development and Redevelopment," p. 72.

5 A Possible Future: The City as a Human Cooperative

1. Sar A. Levitan, Garth L. Mangum, Robert Taggart III, *Economic Opportunity in the Ghetto: The Partnership of Government and Business* (Baltimore and London: The Johns Hopkins Press, 1970).

2. Ramsay Clark, *Crime in America, Observations on Its Nature, Causes, Prevention and Control* (New York: Simon & Schuster, 1970).

3. Loewenstein and Hermann, *San Francisco Community Renewal Program: A Summary*.

4. Frances Fox Piven and Richard Cloward, *Regulating the Poor* (New York: Pantheon Books, 1971).

5. Anthony Downs, "Who Are the Urban Poor?" Supplementary Paper No. 26, Committee for Economic Development, New York, 1970.

6. John Dyckman, *op. cit.*

7. *Model Cities: A Step Towards the New Federalism*, The Report of the President's Task Force on Model Cities, August, 1970, p. 10.

8. Kenneth B. Clark, *Dark Ghetto—Dilemmas of Social Power* (New York, Harper & Row, 1967).

Index

Independent Voters of Illinois, 135
Interior, U. S. Department of, 60
Iron Curtain, 93
Israel, 4
Italy, 122

Japanese, 180
Jefferson County, 130
Jefferson, Thomas, 55
Jencks, Christopher, 18f, 93, 139, 179
Johnson administration, 85, 95
Johnson, Chalmers, 100
Johnson, President Lyndon, 59, 132
Justice Without Trial, 110, 166
Juvenile Delinquency, President's Committee on, 58, 93

Kansas City, 44
Kansas Health Workers, 153, 154
Kaplan, Harold, 43
Kasahara, Yoshiko, 65
Kaufman, Herbert, 91
Kennedy administration, 100
Kennedy plan, 136
Kennedy, Senator Edward, 151
Keynes, John Maynard, 28, 64, 80, 114f
King, Martin Luther, 36
Kinloch, Mo., 48
Koerner, Otto, 128
Kozol, Jonathan, 128
Kristol, Irving, 139

Marx, Karl, 84
Massachusetts Institute of Technology, 82
Massachusetts Turnpike Commission, 131
McCordie, W. J., 43
McLean, Joseph, 56
Medicare, 136, 139, 151
Meltsner, Arnold S., 39
Merriam, Robert, 59
Metropolitan Enigma, 87
Meyerson, Martin, 89
Miami, 29
Miami Metro, 47
Middle Ages, 4, 5
Millcreek, Saint Louis, 132
Miller, S. M., 98, 101
Mill, John Stuart, 126
Milwaukee, Wisconsin, 79
Minar, David, 147, 155
Minneapolis, Minn., 131
Mississippi, 122
Model Cities expediter, 60
Montreal, Canada, 65
Morris, Norval, 109f, 129, 167
Moses, Robert, 131
Moynihan, Daniel P., 64, 68

Nader, Ralph, 37
National Alliance of Businessmen, 160
National Guard, 88
Newark, New Jersey, *vi*, *x*, 115, 174, 183
New Haven, Connecticut, 7, 88, 122, 126, 132
New Jersey, 122
Newman, Dorothy, 98